THE WILDLIFE CONFESSIONAL

Kick It in the Ice Hole and Other Stories

Edited by
Matthew P. Bettelheim and Thomas A. Roberts
(The Wildlife Society—Western Section)

Founded in 1953, the Western Section of The Wildlife Society is a noprofit scientific and educational association dedicated to excellence in wildlife stewardship through science and education. Our mission is to enhance the ability of wildlife professionals and wildlife students to conserve diversity, sustain productivity, and ensure responsible use of wildlife resources and their habitats. In the spirit of education and public engagement, we are proud to offer this anthology to our readers; however, the stories, the experiences, and the views expressed belong solely to the authors and do not necessarily reflect those of The Wildlife Society or the Western Section.

Published by Inkshares, Inc., Oakland, California
www.inkshares.com

Cover design by Matthew Bettelheim
Interior design by Kevin G. Summers

ISBN: 9781947848788
e-ISBN: 9781947848795
LCCN: 2018967132

First edition

Printed in the United States of America

INTRODUCTION

The anthology in your hands is a window into the wildlife profession, a career peopled by wildlife biologists, game wardens, land managers, researchers, students, and the community of peers who have built their careers (and sometimes, their lives) around working with wildlife. Members of the biology community may specialize in a certain group of wildlife—like entomologists (insects), ichthyologists (fish), ornithologists (birds), herpetologists (reptiles and amphibians), and mammalogists (mammals). Or they may practice their "–ology" on a larger scale—like law enforcement, policy, habitat restoration, resource management, research, outreach, and education. However, they all share a passion for wildlife and the outdoors, and a learned (resigned?) resiliency to the pitfalls and mishaps inherent in a career that revolves around wildlife. Anyone who has seen even one nature documentary or watched humming-birds in their backyard feeder has probably entertained the inkling that wildlife can be unpredictable; the only real difference between Jack or Jill Public and a wildlife biologist is that the latter has undoubtedly experienced it firsthand—and probably has a story or two to tell. This anthology is a collection of their stories.

The Wildlife Confessional was conceived by members of The Wildlife Society to serve three primary purposes: (1) to record the oral histories, memories, and experiences of wildlife professionals in a way that promotes collegiality and camaraderie; (2) to recruit, educate, and attract students to the wildlife biology field and The Wildlife Society; and (3) to apply money raised through book sales to support student involvement in the society by funding scholarships, grants, and training opportunities.

The authors whose stories have been collected here represent men and women from all walks of wildlife biology—state and federal biologists, consultants, students, professors, interns—and take place across North and Central America, from the Gulf of Alaska to San Ignacio, Belize; from the tropics of the Hawaiian Islands to the deserts of Arizona; and in the desert springs, coastal bluffs, national parks, stock ponds, pickup trucks, traplines, doctors' offices, rooftops, outhouses, and bombing ranges scattered everywhere in between.

In *Owned by a Pirate Kit Fox*, kit fox expert Brian Cypher recounts the one that got away—a kit fox so formidable and cantankerous, it nearly brought a grown man to tears. On an island, no one can hear you scream; we learn this the hard way in *The Long Drop*, in which Eric Lund must get his hands dirty while stationed on Laysan Island after a gray-backed tern finds itself doing laps in the loo. Islands can also be a place of reflection, as we experience through the eyes of Brianna Williams in *The Tower Colony* during her turn working with breeding seabirds in an abandoned Air Force station radar tower. In *Lost and Found*, J. Drew Lanham looks back on the formative years that shaped his inevitable career as a birder, a path especially rocky for a young African American growing up in South Carolina in the 1970s. In *The Big Horn Sheep De-Watering Device*, veteran author and wildlife biologist Thomas A. Roberts makes a beginner's mistake and pays for it when a three foot-long pipe wrench becomes his cross to bear in a trek across the desert. At the end of her rope, Katie Quint turns to poetry to reflect on *The $#!% I Do for Dave*. After years of managing problem bears, former National Park Service biologist Jeff Keay retraces his footsteps through Yosemite in *Smarter than the Average Bear* to see who is winning the arms race when it comes to bear-proofing our parks to keep the public—and bears—safe. Alone on Chimney Rock during the summer of 1975, fledgling biologist Marcy Cottrell Houle writes with grit and grace about her experience studying one of the seven last pairs of wild peregrines surviving in the Rocky Mountains in *Wings for My Flight*, excerpted from Houle's award-winning novel by the same name. When it rains bullets and beer cans on his first day of work, getting stuck in the mud becomes the least of Joseph Drake's worries during the eventful evening of *The First Day*. In *Bender Springs*, Drake trades the woods for a white-knuckle summer dodging unexploded ordnances and drug smugglers to inventory the deserts' tinajas. In *A Terrible Bird Is the Pelican*, Ivan Parr is blinded by new insight into why terror remains a thing with feathers. After an owl call goes wrong, Darren Sleep finds his calling in *You Never Forget Your First*, an homage to night owlers and their quarry. Wildlife biologist Matthew Bettelheim looks back at his years spent in pursuit of the burrow-dwelling California tiger salamander in *Seeing Spots: Field Notes from the Underground*, and then reflects on his years in the field with a top-ten list of sorts that shows how little he's learned in *Ticks, Quails, and Pollywog Tails—That's What Wildlife Biologists Are Made of, or Several Habits of a Highly Effective Wildlifer*. When Charles Jonkel is given the rare opportunity to pioneer the first ever study of polar bears in the Arctic, little does he know that the years to follow will not only change how the world sees polar bears, but will also leave him looking back at those years to wonder how he survived the experience in *Kick It in the Ice Hole*.

To illustrate *The Wildlife Confessional*'s cover—itself a good-natured nod to The Wildlife Society's professional journal, *The Wildlife Professional*—San Francisco Bay Area photographer Sarah Anne Bettelheim captured the spirit of the project with a toad and a pair of boots set against the backdrop of St. Teresa of Avila, the iconic Bodega, California, church established in 1862. If it looks familiar, that could be because it was made famous by photographer Ansel Adams in 1953. From *The Wildlife Confessional*'s inception, this photograph has become the banner around which our contributing authors have gathered to share their adventures. And to bring the stories behind *The Wildlife Confessional* to life, anthology contributor Ivan Parr (*A Terrible Bird Is the Pelican*)—who is also gainfully employed as a wildlife biologist, botanist, and nature photographer—put pen to paper a second time. But this time around, Ivan set out to create the lighthearted illustrations that accompany each story. If a picture is worth a thousand words, Ivan's art speaks volumes about the wildlife profession and the adventures wildlife biologists face every day.

We endeavor to show the humor and poignancy in the day-to-day adventures that define and enlighten us—or that, sometimes, we'd rather forget. These are the yarns we tell over a campfire or a cold beer or a long car ride. These are our adventures, misadventures, revelations, reflections, mishaps, and pivotal experiences with wildlife in the field. These pages are our wildlife confessional.

The Editors
Matthew P. Bettelheim   Thomas A. Roberts

IN LOVING MEMORY OF
THOMAS A. ROBERTS

The Wildlife Confessional was first conceived many moons ago, long before I began exchanging emails in 2014 with co-editor Thomas A. Roberts about an idea I had for an anthology. My first introduction to Tom was more than ten years earlier, when a friend loaned me a copy of Tom's very own anthology, *Painting the Cows* (1998). At that time, I had just joined the ranks of an elite group of scientists known as "wildlife biologists" and was interning at *Bay Nature* magazine, so a collection of stories about wildlife biology seemed a natural fit. It was. Instantly in love with Tom's brand of self-effacing honesty and insight, I hungrily devoured *Painting the Cows* and its companion anthology, *Adventures in Conservation* (1989), and then loaned my copies out to friends and colleagues until one day I realized my books hadn't found their way home.

In 2005, I lucked into Tom's email address and reached out to him about meeting for drinks, hopeful to meet another local writer/wildlife biologist—but because it is too easy to get swept up in the current of everyday life, despite several emails back and forth, we never made it happen. And then in 2007, at a happy hour for our local San Francisco Bay Area Chapter of The Wildlife Society, I heard someone mention "Tom Roberts" and realized that Tom Roberts—*the* Tom Roberts—was sitting at the next table over. So, I did what any normal person might do when faced with a "celebrity crush" and rushed over to introduce myself and heap praise on his work, coming across no doubt as a babbling fool in the process.

A friend at Tom's table that night later confided to me that Tom had been moved to tears by my fawning. I don't regret my tomfoolery (if you will pardon the pun) for one minute. By the time the pieces began falling into place in 2014 for the anthology you now hold in your hands, Tom Roberts seemed the natural person to reach out to as a co-collaborator. And then *The Wildlife Confessional* was born. Together, we waded through more than forty-five submissions to carefully curate the fifteen stories bound together here.

But even happy coincidences can come to a sad conclusion, and such was the case with Tom. In late 2016, Tom was forced to put his pen aside after a yearlong battle with Parkinson's disease. And on November 24, 2017, at the age of seventy, Tom Roberts passed away. Although *Painting the Cows* and *Adventures in Conservation* are out of print today, you will find Tom's favorite story—"The Bighorn Sheep De-Watering Device"—in this collection. And so, even if you didn't have the pleasure of knowing Tom in life, this story will surely help you get acquainted, and—if nothing else—remember him running through the desert in his skivvies clutching an eighteen-and-a-half-pound wrench.

Matthew P. Bettelheim
Concord, California
March 2018

CONTENTS

OWNED BY A PIRATE KIT FOX

Brian Cypher, CWB
Research Ecologist, Endangered Species Recovery Program
California State University–Stanislaus

It has been said that I am a kit fox expert. To this day, I'm not sure I know what that means. I've always suspected it was a title earned with equal parts longevity and experience. In my case, I suspect I joined the "expert" club by virtue of persistence—clearly, that's what happens when you mess with something long enough (two decades, if anyone's counting).

However I got here, I must give myself credit for attaining some level of proficiency in handling the little guys. Handling kit foxes isn't a macho thing like gator wrestling or wrangling rattlesnakes or jumping on the backs of large ungulates caught in nets. Kit foxes can be as large as a house cat, but most barely exceed 2–2.5 kg (4.5–5.5 lbs.). Despite their diminutive stature, they can be lightning-quick and have extremely sharp teeth. Thus, a certain level of expertise is required to ensure that both the fox and the handler complete the process unscathed. The safety of the fox becomes especially important when I'm working with the San Joaquin kit fox (*Vulpes macrotis mutica*), a federally endangered and state-listed threatened species in California.

Although today I consider myself sufficiently competent and adept at handling kit foxes, this was not always the case. In the beginning, there was one fox that "owned" me. He was a 2.5-kg ball of nastiness that for nearly a year caused me untold stress and anxiety, made me fearful of showing up for work, and gave me nightmares. And this is our story.

In July of 1990, I moved to Bakersfield, California, in the southern San Joaquin Valley. I had just completed my doctoral degree at Southern Illinois University working on coyotes and had been offered a position with a company that was contracted by the Department of Energy to conduct extensive research and monitoring of listed species at the then government-owned Elk Hills oil field in Kern County. Now, my passion and professional desire had long been to work with wild canids. In the early years of my budding career, I had already worked with gray wolves, coyotes, red foxes, and gray foxes. This new job offered an opportunity to work extensively with yet another species, the San Joaquin kit fox. Even better, the position offered a living wage instead of the ramen noodle wages I had earned as a technician or graduate student! I jumped at the opportunity.

My first day of work coincided with the beginning of the "summer intensive trapping session." Since 1980, my company had conducted intensive trapping sessions across the summer and winter to census kit fox abundance. The resulting data were analyzed with a mark-recapture program to produce a population estimate. In brief, our 147-square-mile study area was covered by thirty traplines of fourteen to sixteen traps each. Trap locations were spaced approximately a quarter mile apart along each line, and a wire-cage box trap was set at each location. One person operated each line and traps were checked four consecutive mornings. It took six weeks for our staff to complete all thirty lines.

The summer sessions were the worst. During San Joaquin Valley's intense summer heat, we could only open and bait traps after 4:30 p.m., a condition of our permits to prevent exposing trapped animals to high temperatures for prolonged periods of time before sunset. At 5:00 a.m., we began checking the traps again to make sure they were all closed and that the foxes were processed and released no later than two hours after sunrise. Because most of the staff, including me, lived one hour away in Bakersfield, this meant waking up at 3:30 a.m. and not getting home before 7:30 p.m. Although in principle there were separate crews to open and close, all bets were off if you were the new guy. And I was the new guy.

Typically, the crew that opened the traps consisted of people who were not trained to handle foxes and most of them never would be (e.g., student interns, botanists, etc.). Because I wasn't yet trained, I was initially assigned to this crew. But I was hired to be, among other things, a fox handler, and so I was asked to work both crews until my training was completed. I had a hard time saying no. I went with little sleep for four nights each week: up at 3:30 a.m., closed traps, opened traps, returned home, ate a quick meal, showered, slept for a few hours, repeat. Those first weeks were rough.

In my past field positions, the mammals I had worked with were much larger than kit foxes. In most instances, I had handled these animals using chemical immobilization. When the San Joaquin kit fox handling method was first described to me, I was understandably anxious. No drugs were used. This wild animal with fox-fast reflexes and predator's teeth would be fully awake and alert while we processed them.

If everything went according to textbook, "processing" a kit fox typically looked something like this: Once caught, the fox was coaxed into a heavy denim bag wrapped around one end of the trap. The fox was then physically restrained on the ground through the bag while the handler carefully exposed various body parts to collect necessary data. The handler's first stop was a careful inspection of the fox's rear end to determine gender and assess reproductive status. Then, a hind-foot measurement was taken, followed by exposing the ears to collect measurements and to insert a metal tag in one ear. At this point, the neck was also accessible if a radio collar was necessary.

And that was the easy part.

With the fox firmly under control, the handler next exposed the entire head to examine the eyes and teeth. Between the physical restraint and dark interior of the bag, most foxes remained relatively quiet and docile up to this point. But as soon as their eyes were exposed and they saw daylight, many tried to bolt. If your grip wasn't firm, they could blow out of the bag and escape before you were done processing them. Assuming the fox hadn't escaped by then, a tooth exam was conducted by carefully inserting a "tooth stick" crossways into the fox's mouth (so that one end of the stick protruded on each side of the fox's mouth) and working it back toward their molars to help hold the jaw agape. If everything went smoothly, the handler could clearly examine the fox's mouth for tooth wear or signs of injury. With the examination complete, the sides of the bag were peeled back and the fox was given its freedom. All in all, it was a slick process and completely bypassed the hassle and risk associated with drugging an animal.

I was admittedly skeptical about the no-drug policy at first. But, I reasoned, I was the new guy. Handlers before me had followed this method for more than ten years before my happy face had shown up.

According to training protocol, I first had to observe experienced handlers in the field, and I did so in the days that followed. The whole process seemed simple enough. And not once did a handler come close to getting mauled by a fox.

When it was my turn to give it a try, I bagged the fox with little effort. Or so I thought—until it wiggled its head out of the bag. Without thinking, I grabbed at the fox and with the help of my trainer, Greg, we worked it back into the bag. Greg explained afterward that reaching as I had for an escaping fox was a sure way to get bitten. I had narrowly dodged a mauling. It went as well as could be expected for a rookie as we finished processing that fox and the next few. But it was clear to me I was still struggling to keep control of the foxes. My previous experience with *larger* canids was working *against* me! I was afraid that I was going to break these little guys. I simply wasn't gripping them as firmly as I needed to. In those first few weeks, a couple of foxes escaped my grasp prematurely. I had usually collected most of the data and tagged them before they would explode from the bag as I went to expose their head. Adept or smooth I was not.

A trainee needed to handle ten foxes with a trainer before they were considered "trained." By week five of the six-week summer session, I was nearly there. Then came the fateful day. I and my trainer du jour, a gal who had scarcely more experience than I, had just finished processing my tenth fox. As I was collecting our gear, she had run back to our truck and—unbeknownst to me—radioed a colleague (recall, this was 1990—cell phones were still some fantasy of the future!).

I made it back to the truck, loaded the gear, and jumped into the driver's seat. We were on our way to the next trap when a fellow biologist who was working the adjacent trapline crossed our path. I knew (as did the entire staff) that he and my trainer were in a romantic relationship. Even so, it came as a surprise when, as I pulled our truck alongside his to chat, my trainer said, "Okay, you are now trained. See ya," jumped out of my truck and into her beau's, and they drove off. So be it, but there were still traps to be checked.

Flying solo, I had only made it three traps down Trap Line 21 before I came across my first fox. I didn't know it at the time, but my first solo fox would prove to be *the* fox. Not yet in the know, my neophyte self with less-than-confident fox handling skills thought *Okay, I've got this* as I laid out my gear and went to bag up my first fox. I may have been green, but two things struck me rather quickly as I approached that trap. The first thing I noticed as I sized up the fox (a male, as I would come to learn) was that his left eye was "squinty" to the point of almost being closed. Also, his left upper lip was pulled up just slightly in a sneer. Together, these beauty marks suggested a resemblance to a pirate. And this was not far off the mark because the second thing that struck me was the ear-piercing, snarling scream. Most foxes never make a sound as they are being manhandled during processing. Some will make a soft *roop, roop* sound, which is an anxiety vocalization. But this fox's scream was bloodcurdling. He made it clear from the start that he was not going to be the textbook timid or compliant fox that I had become accustomed to during my short initiation.

Things only got worse when I went to maneuver the trap to get him into the bag. Not only did he continue to scream, but he also flung himself and snapped jaws at wherever I touched the trap. Tentatively, I worked the bag over the mouth of the trap and—carefully opening the trapdoor through the bag—I blew on him, banged on the sides of the trap, and feigned rushes at him to work him into the bag. Each move was met with a scream and a snap. This went on for several minutes until I began to feel panicked and fatigued. I was beginning to consider letting him go—the ultimate failure of a handler—when, still snarling and snapping, he finally backed into the bag.

All along, I had thought (hoped?!) that, once in the bag, the fox would calm down and settle like most foxes did when they were bagged. But any hopes for normalcy were immediately dashed. I might as well have bagged the Tasmanian Devil. Even in the bag, he continued to scream and spin around in the sack like a whirling dervish. Usually, we would hold the bag up and feel around to determine where the back and front ends of the fox were. But every time I touched the bag, he would immediately spin around and bite at the spot. I was holding a five-pound bag of canid hell that wanted nothing more (other than to get away) than to open up a can o' whup-ass on me! I didn't know what to do.

Becoming desperate, it came to me suddenly that I might be able use the wooden tooth stick to focus his attention. When I poked at the bag with the stick, the fox whirled around and latched on to it through the heavy denim. But now, I could clearly see where his head was and I dropped to the ground with the bag and scruffed him by the neck. Still, nothing went smoothly. Despite my best efforts to restrain and control the fox, I might as well have been riding a rodeo bull. I was barely able to check his hindquarters to confirm his gender, but was successful in inserting the all-important ear tag. But as soon as he saw daylight, he exploded out of my grasp. For a split

second, I feared he was going to come back for my whup-ass. But like many foxes, he stopped a few feet away and stared back at me. The only difference was, this pirate fox managed to give me an incredible vulpine stink eye with his one good eye before he turned and trotted off into the saltbush.

The whole encounter left me shaken and soaked with sweat. But there were still traps to check and I finished the trapline that day without encountering another fox. By day's end, I felt thrashed. I've never been much of a drinker, but that morning a tall drink sure sounded like a good idea.

And maybe I should have had that drink, because the pirate kit fox was back in the same trap the next day. *What the hell?!* I wondered despondently as I prepared myself for battle. *Didn't you have enough fun terrorizing me yesterday? Are you that hard up for canned mackerel?* The processing didn't go much smoother than the day before. This time, however, I knew what to expect, and I didn't have to worry about ear-tagging him. I got him in the bag and took full advantage of the tooth stick trick. But as soon as he saw daylight, I lost what little control I had and he escaped. In no way was I feeling like a competent canid handler. And the next day, to my horror, there he was again. In the same trap. We went through the same stressful, humiliating procedure that ended with him escaping. This fox clearly had my number and seemed—dare I say—to be enjoying himself. Thank Leopold, he was nowhere to be seen on the fourth and last day for Trap Line 21. I didn't for a minute think his absence was an act of pity on my behalf—more likely he tired of me since I had offered so little challenge. He owned me and he knew it.

By the end of the summer session, I had handled fifteen to twenty foxes. Most of them were relatively calm and mellow, nothing like my pirate fox. In late November, we started the winter session. It wasn't uncommon for staff to be assigned traplines they had run previously because it was assumed they were familiar with the trap sites and could work the lines more efficiently. As it turned out, I was assigned Trap Line 21 with the pirate fox. I didn't dwell too much about the fox, although I would be lying if I didn't admit he was on the back of my mind. With turnover from death by predators or natural causes, shifts in individual home ranges, and random chance, I figured *my* chances were good the pirate fox wouldn't be back to terrorize me. But as I approached the infamous trap my first day back on Trap Line 21, there he was! Déjà vu turned to dread combined with a sudden pressing urge to evacuate my bowels. *Damn!* As we faced off with only the trap between us, either the wind or my imagination running amok whispered in my ear, "Aaaarrrrr . . . we meet again, matey!" Resigned, I let the games begin.

He was his same ol' snarling, snapping, screaming self. I bagged, grabbed, and processed him without injury. But he still escaped before I had finished the examination. I tucked my tail between my legs, finished the line, and returned to my office.

I mentioned the fox and its behavior to some coworkers. They laughed and chalked it up to rookie inexperience. Kristie, a colleague who'd made handling foxes look as easy as handling stuffed animals, had a particularly good time razzing me.

Sure enough, the pirate fox was back in the same trap on day two. I muddled through the procedure, but this time I restrained him long enough to get a partial look at his teeth. He gave me the next day off, mercifully, but was back in the trap on day four. It just so happened that Kristie had finished her line early that morning and had come over to lend a hand. She watched as I went through the process with the fox. Afterward she admitted, "That one's an outlier. He's got some anger issues." I walked away feeling a little better about myself that day.

As the winter session wound down, I had racked up thirty to thirty-five handles, and my confidence was on the upswing. We didn't trap again until the following May, when we surveyed natal den areas. There, we captured adult females to assess their reproductive success and captured and tagged pups to assess juvenile survival. This session gave me another fifteen to twenty handles. Working with pups is about as fun as it sounds—they're gentle, mellow, small, cute. It's the kind of experience where you feel like you should be paying to do it instead of getting paid.

And it was that spring that something happened. It had taken me longer than I cared for, but something finally clicked. I finally got it. During those weeks, I had figured out how to deal with difficult foxes, to the point where I actually began to look forward to them.

Before I knew it, the summer session was upon us. When the time came, I specifically requested Trap Line 21, hoping that the pirate fox would show up again. Once again, he obliged on day one and was waiting for me in his usual trap. As I approached the trap, he did not disappoint and regressed immediately into his trademark screaming, snarling, and snapping. *Let the fun begin!* I thought.

A veteran now, I had learned how to better maneuver the shade tarp that covered each trap and blow on the foxes to work them out of the cage. Another trick I had picked up was to set the bagged fox down to let the loose material collapse around the fox. This not only helped restrict their movements, it also presented a clear outline of the fox—particularly the business end with the sharp weapons—making it easier to scruff them. Quickly, I had him positioned under me. I had also gained a much better feel for where and how much pressure to exert to comfortably restrain the fox without causing it discomfort.

With these superpowers at my fingertips, I actually took my time that day. I lifted his hind end up and checked everything thoroughly. Then I turned the bag around and examined his ears, looked for fleas, and felt around his neck and thoracic area to check his overall health. To be sure, he continued to struggle and snarl, but this time with little effect. Then came time to uncover his eyes. Upholding tradition, he made a great effort to get his legs under him and bolt, but he went nowhere. I gave him a scratch between his ears, and then examined his eyes. His pirate eye was still very squinty, but otherwise it looked okay. I could see then that it must have been a scar from an old injury that had healed without any detrimental effects. Using my tooth stick as intended, I took a good look at each tooth and the condition of his gums. He still managed to pepper my tooth stick with tooth marks, but that seemed an acceptable compromise. When I was finished and satisfied with my examination, I let him go. As he had in the past, he stopped about ten feet away, turned, and stared at me with his pirate-like glare.

"There, that wasn't so bad, was it?" I responded.

After a few seconds, he turned and melted into the saltbush.

That was the last I saw of the pirate fox. He didn't show up the rest of the week, nor in any subsequent trapping session. I hope he lived a long life. The reality is, most kit foxes only make it three or four years in the wild. Usually, their end comes in the jaws of a coyote. It's strictly a competitive interaction, since coyotes rarely eat much, if any, of a fox carcass. However, if he met his final demise, I'd like to think the pirate kit fox passed along his genes (and attitude) to numerous offspring. Not only will that help them survive a world full of dangers, but also because there will be plenty of young biologists after me who may end up with one of those swashbuckling progenies in a trap. And those biologists will surely benefit from the huge dose of humility they're dealt and will hopefully gain an appreciation along the way for how much power and chutzpah can be packed into a five-pound fox.

ABOUT THE AUTHOR

BRIAN CYPHER's *primary professional interest is the ecology and conservation of wild canids. However, he enjoys working with a variety of species, many of which are endangered, and include several species of kangaroo rats, pocket mice, antelope squirrels, shrews, and even rare plants, particularly the Bakersfield cactus. For the past twenty-six years, his work has been centered in the San Joaquin Valley. Brian resides in the utopian city of Bakersfield with his wife, Ellen. After a few more years, they look forward to retiring to greener pastures (literally) in northwest Washington, although Brian will likely make frequent trips back south to check on the kit foxes he's become so attached to. Brian has been a member of The Wildlife Society since 1980. He is a Certified Wildlife Biologist, has served as an associate editor of the* Journal of Wildlife Management, *and was appointed a Wildlife Society Fellow for exceptional service to the wildlife profession in 2014.*

A TERRIBLE BIRD IS THE PELICAN

Ivan Parr
Senior Biologist, AECOM

One afternoon, a pelican poked me in the eyeball. I wasn't angry at the time. But now, if I ever see that pelican again, I'll make him rue the day he was taken off the endangered species list. I am aware that pelicans have no concept of Federal legislation (if any bird did, it would be a corvid, and that would be disastrous). I am also aware that unless you are a three-year-old, your assailant is a maniacal urban goose, and you were just saying "hi," you should never blame the bird in a bird-on-human injury. So, allow me to make a de facto point in the pelican's defense. Perhaps he came from a troubled nest on the rough side of the guano rock. Maybe his father stole from fishing lines, and his mother premasticated baitfish, favoring a mean bigger sister with a fuzzy topknot. Or it was El Nino, and discarded minnow heads were the best a family with four horrifically ugly chicks could live on. Who knows? But in *my* defense, no nonfictional person should have to walk this world fearing an attack by a bird.

Throughout modern history, *Homo sapiens* has enjoyed the impunity to hunt, eat, and harass birds. Consider that chicken is the most consumed meat in the Western Hemisphere, followed by beef. Then consider that there's no such thing as a death-defying "running of the roosters." Unlike the perils associated with cattle, or, for that matter, the apex predators of other vertebrate classes—lions, crocodiles, and sharks—we have generally avoided being eaten, beaten, or crushed by eagles, ravens, and gulls. When modern bird-watchers emerged in western culture, opera glasses and rifles were replaced by scopes and binoculars. Throughout that transition, the most dangerous thing a bird enthusiast encountered was one's partner. Birding remains as innocuous as philately and only as dangerous as one's obsession. In our cushy Holocene times, the thought of a bird harming a human is fantastical—even comical.

Yet, if prehistoric bird-watching had been in vogue as recently as 2.8 million years ago, the sport would have involved more running and hiding than squinting and squabbling. Back then, twitching might have been as leisurely as hawk-watching is for squirrels today. No elders on an Audubon Society field trip have fussed over whether it's a *Kelenken* or a *Brontornis*—both seven-to-ten-foot-tall "terror birds" of the Miocene. These, along with the more recent North American *Titanis walleri*, are theorized to have been apex predators, capable of taking down large mammals. So, while the opportunity has gone the way of the dodo, there could have been a time when birds were capable of preying on humans—had we been available. A few even lasted into human history, but of these, we've literally outgrown our fear of the crowned eagle (*Stephanoaetus coronatus*), and sent the Maori-terrorizing Haast's eagle (*Harpagornis moorei*) to extinction.

The modern birder has it easy.

By that same reasoning, the modern birder has the short end of the stick. For the last sixty million years, bird diversity has evolved like Apple products, favoring smaller, smarter, noisier models that are easily lost, obsessively tracked, and confounding to listen to. As technology has dispensed of Babbage's Difference Engine, so has the natural world replaced the demon duck of doom (*Bullockornis planei*) with innumerable Little Brown Jobbers, or LBJs. Fantails (*Rhipidura fuliginosa*) persist where moas (Dinornithiformes) have vanished. Kinglets (*Regulus*) and wrens (Troglodytidae) fill the old haunts of monstrous *Bathornis* and *Paracrax*. Name any terrestrial niche, and there's a passerine for that, pooping purple berries on your car and chitter-chattering an insult on their magnificent *Coelurosaurian* ancestors who flew the coop before humans could enjoy them.

The story is not totally bleak. One bird still thriving in the Americas lives up to its Oligocene glory: a dinosaur that has hardly changed in thirty million years. Human history is but a blink in the existence of the pelican, whose ancestors saw the first felids and watched continents tear apart. And while incomparable to *Titanis*, the pelican does rain terror down on any living thing that fits in its mouth—not just fish, but lizards, frogs, lobsters, gannets, chickens, rodents, pigeons, ducks (and, if the internet is to be believed, cats, dogs, bears, donkeys, and people. Note: the internet is not to be believed).

More than an opportunistic predator, the pelican is enchanting. I have spent many sunsets watching formations of Pterosaurian pelicans returning to roost. Their aerial and diving displays are spellbinding. When a brown pelican glides overhead, the *whoosh* of its great silver wings evokes, for me, nostalgia unmatched by any other bird. With its fiddleneck head, amused frown, expressive blue eyes, and that centurion galea crest of stiff chestnut feathers, for what other bird do people ask as often, "Is that a pterodactyl?"

Despite its Pterosaurian body plan, humans have never questioned the pelican's identity. To us, a pelican is more a pelican than a rose a rose, or even a flamingo a flamingo. The genus, family, and order share the prefix "pelican," demonstrating our acknowledgment of its taxonomic distinctiveness at many levels. This bird is so unambiguously "pelican" that the term has barely changed since classical times and, unlike most other bird families, all species share one name—a word with no English synonym that I have heard.

This is not because the pelican fails to inspire imagination. Human fascination with the pelican knows no bounds. This bird is a motif in Aboriginal and Incan folklore and art. It is the self-sacrificing parent that symbolizes the Eucharist in the Christian faith. In ancient Egypt, it is the Goddess Henet who protects the dead on their way to the Afterlife. It's the state bird of Louisiana, commemorated in its state nickname, and is claimed as the national bird of Romania, Barbados, Saint Maarten, and Saint Kitts and Nevis. The pelican is on the seals of at least two universities and serves as mascot for another. It lends its moniker to titles from celebrated authors like John Grisham and Katherine Paterson, not to mention a book publisher. Elite luggage, coolers, cases, kayaks, boats, water systems, furniture, headlamps, java books, a pizza franchise, a clothing line, a farming business, a credit union, a solar company, and even a basketball team pay homage to the pelican, as do innumerable lakes, beaches, peaks, keys, bays, and resorts. It is one of only three birds portrayed by Geoffrey Rush in mainstream film[1]; and finally and fittingly, its name is borne by two notorious prisons: Alcatraz and Pelican Bay.

[1] Geoffrey Rush played a pigeon in *The Man Who Could Not Dream*, an owl in *The Guardians of Ga'Hoole*, and Nigel the Pelican in *Finding Nemo*.

On top of all this, the pelican is easy pickings for a photographer. Luckily for a Californian, the fashionable California brown pelican (*Pelecanus occidentalis californicus*)—a subspecies that sports a bright red-and-olive throat pouch during the breeding season—is the most photogenic of its North American congeners: beautiful, yet approachable. Or, so I used to think.

* * *

It was spring 2009. I'd just gotten over a bout of poison oak that had sealed up my right eye like a chayote. Finally able to drive, I headed to Monterey, California, for seabird photography—an annual pastime. My recovery was well timed. I was due to leave the country the following day.

Pelicans are easy to find in the right season. In just a minute's stroll down Fisherman's Wharf, I spied one nabbing fish from a gutting station down where the *Sea Wolf* is docked. He sported a shaggy coat of frayed paisley, dark eyes glinting from the oil of his prey, and a Mohawk that said, *I just don't give a ratfish's caudal peduncle.* His roguish smile told of the Heermann's gulls he'd kicked in the undertail coverts. His supercilious brow mocked whatever hope some pelican-ignorant recluse might fancy in a thing with feathers. Yes, he was the meanest bird on the dock as he stood, but nothing said it better than the blue band on his leg.

Apart from serving as pelican bling, the blue band meant that he'd been rehabilitated and released by International Bird Rescue (IBR). IBR encourages citizens to report the band numbers so they can keep track of their releases. They even host a contest. So, when I spotted the pelican, I went down to read his tag.

Blue-band the Pelican was unafraid. Pacing back and forth along the cleaning stations, he stalked fishermen hoisting their catch onto the wharf. As they tried to shoo him, shadows dappled the dock and a pod of ten or so pelicans descended onto the pile of fish guts. United as one unwieldy hydra, the pirates rubbed shoulder to shoulder for the plunder. Pouches bulging, necks twisting, throats wriggling with fish, and heads rising and falling like oil donkeys, they exercised their endangered right. The exasperated fishermen turned toward the wharf above and called out to some IBR staff or volunteers who hurried down to the dock and chased the freeloaders off with flappy motions. A hand pressed to the bill of Blue-band knocked him off his perch to circle high above us. But as soon as the IBR people turned their backs, Blue-band landed on the nearest piling to steal live rockfish from a bucket. I decided to make a pest out of myself by photographing him.

"Can you get rid of him?" a fisherman asked me, backing away from the bird's fixated stare. "He's up to no good."

"Sure . . ." I replied, stalling to take more shots.

I don't know why the fisherman had asked *me* to do it, but I also didn't want to habituate a pelican any more than the next biologist. Copying the IBR guy from a minute before, I put my hand against the enormous lever handle that is a pelican's face, and shoved the bird off his piling. Spreading out his six-foot tapestry of shaggy-chic, Blue-band flapped toward me. One of his primaries scraped across my right eyeball as he struggled to gain airflow. Then he launched off to rob a dinghy.

Against a setting sun, a pelican's wings are silver-plated emblems of eternity. On a fish-gutting station, a pelican's wings are slime-coated bristle broom. So, when the bird's wingtips scratched my cornea, I was more disgusted than pained. But I washed out my eye, got over it, and boarded a plane for Belize the next morning.

* * *

Home base in Belize was a property owned and run by friends Vance and Jody Bente in the hills of San Ignacio. The property housed the eco-lodge Casa del Caballo Blanco (CDCB), as well as a bird rehabilitation hospital and a passive restoration project collectively known as the Casa Avian Support Alliance, or CASA. CASA has been closed and dormant since 2011, but during its tenure, two other friends—herpetologists Jeff Alvarez and Wendy Dexter—had been involved in monitoring the restoration site. As the newcomer, I had been appointed botanist. In addition to our restoration monitoring responsibilities, our directive was to establish CASA's presence at the country's first ever meeting of the Belize Wildlife Conservation Network held at Galen University. This event was attended by some of the country's top biologists, educators, veterinarians, landholders, and officials from the Department of Environment. During our stay, Jeff, Wendy, and I squeezed in some wild-life watching on the side. We visited a Mennonite farm where a little girl used a dead mouse on a string to play with the Morelet's crocodile in her family's pond. We birded with Ricky Manzanero, Belize's Master Birder and CDCB's groundskeeper. We also spent an evening herping on the grounds. The fearless but careful Jeff Alvarez caught many herpetological treasures. We handled irritant-coated cane toads, milky tree frogs, Gulf Coast toads, tarantulas, and most notably, a terrestrial snail sucker (*Sibon sartorii*). And we volunteered our time cleaning cages at CASA's bird hospital, where specialist Tracy Anderson tirelessly treated and exercised the avian patients.

All of these activities were named potential culprits when I woke up one morning with an aching eyeball.

The rainforest gloom peeping through the ceiling vents felt like a plasma cutter splicing my retina. My eye had become so sensitive overnight, when I stepped into the daylight, the entire right side of my face scrunched like a poked anemone, the lachrymal oozing in tears. My good eye, the left eye, con-stricted by proximity so I had to pry it open with my forefinger and thumb to see my way to the breakfast room. Here, Wendy helped me administer a saline solution, but not before having to force open my eye using "the death grip."

This solution worked well enough that I was able to attend the conference with Wendy, Jeff, and Jody. A twenty-three-year-old official from the Department of the Environment was among the first speakers that day. In the middle of her pre-sentation, the anguish so swiftly and violently returned that the official looked straight at me—and laughed. She must've thought I was making faces at her. After that, I used a handker-chief to cover my distorted mug. Even then, the ducts would gush and the retina would shrivel like a salted slug when a glint through the clouds showered razors through the sore eyelid. I became accustomed to holding my hand over the eye—making glasses useless (they were broken anyway)—so that I had to use a contact lens in my one good eye, a detail that would become critical in the days ahead.

"Boy, you are *hurting*," Ricky observed when I wasn't able to look up to see a yellow-naped parrot. My friends suggested that I see a specialist. During lunch, Shenny—Ricky's daughter and one of the staff at CDCB—drove me to a doctor in San Ignacio. Curtains were drawn, lights were dimmed, but the light of an ophthalmoscope set my optic nerves on fire. A lame duck in a dark room, I listened to my polyglot friend interpret what the blurry, mustached doctor murmured. Rendering my disobedient eyelids asunder with his hands, the doctor said something Shenny did not need to translate: "¡Dios mío . . . que asqueroso!"—"My God . . . that's nasty!"

The doctor prescribed me a vial of something bleary, and we went back to CASA. Once administered, the liquid felt like a poisonous brain freeze, and I saw stars. I wasn't surprised when Tracy picked up the vial and asked, "He gave you THIS!? We were banned from using this on *BIRDS* five years ago!" Into the trash it went, and instead I made do by repeatedly numbing my eyes with something Tracy had in the bird hospital that was up to code.

The enclosed CASA bird hospital was one of the few dark places I could get respite. And now that I was at the bird hospital taking bird medicine, I got to chat with the other birds in the ward. Parrots and ramphastids, who've pulled more than their weight by bringing coolness to the neoaves, make great company. And yet, I could not stop watching the wild species that came to snag moths off the walls and cock their heads at the cage-bound convalescents. These freeloaders were nothing special, just the same insipid passerines I'd disparaged back home. The more I watched, the more curious I became of the robotic warbler and the sparrow with its sewing machine mandibles.

Here I stood on the Pan-American land bridge, the migratory funnel for millions of tiny songbirds, like the blue-gray gnatcatcher and the Wilson's warbler. The same land bridge brought us *Titanis walleri*, migrating on foot over generations, but these little brown-and-yellow jobbers were crossing from South to Central to North America and back again annually. Passing between two continents around me was a greater number and diversity of little songsters than I had the capacity to appreciate. I grew mad with frustration trying to identify tanagers flitting in the eye-scorching canopies above. What made them so interesting now, when many of the same birds move through my backyard? Was it the forced perspective of a one-eyed birder?

My eye's sensitivity worsened, but when your human companions are as stalwart as mine were, you deal with it. One-eyed and one-legged birds at CASA could cope. So, if the world looked like a vintage View-Master slide through the slit of my aching "good" eye, I could still enjoy the beauty of Belize.

Birds were everywhere. The conference brought up strategies to save orange-breasted falcons, snake-eagles, Harpy eagles, and macaws. I wanted to see them all, but watching the sky was like pointing a spotting scope at the sun. No eye patch presented itself, so I made do with hankies, napkins, my hand, or a pair of ladies' black underwear (long story) and went off on further adventures with Wendy, Jeff, and Tracy.

Dinner one night found us discussing the evolution and survival strategies of birds. Someone brought up the well-supported theory that the Taung Child (the fossilized skull of a young *Australopithecus africanus* hominid discovered in South Africa in 1924) had been a victim of an eagle, spur-ring a debate as to whether a contemporary eagle could take a *Homo sapiens*. There is, in fact, some evidence suggesting modern bird-watchers between the ages of three and seven could still be eaten by the crowned eagle and a select number of extant predatory birds.

From there, Tracy segued into the often-dangerous personalities of birds she'd rehabbed during her career in Belize, the States, and Canada. The elegant heron could turn dagger-wielding ingrate. Beautiful parrots? Finger-biting troublemakers. And then, there was the brown pelican. Feisty, demanding, and unafraid, stoic and strong.

"But also elegant, beautiful, maybe intelligent," we agreed.

At that point, Vance looked at me and asked, "But didn't you say, the other day, that a pelican . . ." and I finally put two and two together as we both finished the sentence, ". . . poked you in *the eye!*"

Elegant, beautiful, intelligent, my right eye! That pelican, that dirty, rotten, no-good, smelly gas bag! Yes, gas bag! Pelicans are festooned with little air sacs—they can't deny it! I was an idiot to forget the Day of the Pelican. The four and a half days I spent in Belize felt like a year, so that fraction of a second when remige-number-nine grazed my eye felt as distant as *Titanis walleri*, and every bit as horrible.

I wasn't prepared for my Pelican Eye (as my friends dubbed it) to occupy the next five months of my life. Returning home from Belize, I began a long saga of eye treatments, most of which made things worse. After weeks of failed experiments with various ophthalmologists, a coworker recommended the services of Dr. Eyeball.

I scheduled a visit for the following week, but the pain worsened so that by that very afternoon, I couldn't even wait for a taxi. Clutching my steering wheel in one hand and using the other to pry my better eye open, I played chicken with San Francisco Bay Area traffic. Just as an owl's affixed eyes makes it necessary to swivel its head, I had to throw my head left and right for my pinhead viewfinder of an eye to piece together a photoplay of the flashing surrounds. Equally owl-like were my chances of going from oblivion to obliteration at the hands of oncoming traffic. Here, a merging car appeared, there a pedestrian, here a light, there I screeched to a halt. Luck, a tight grip, and the mercy of my fellow drivers got me across town. I landed diagonally in the parking lot and ran down to the doctor's office.

The doctor saw me that afternoon, but I not him. My right eye was unopenable, and my sunny adventures as Mr. Magoo had exhausted my left to dysfunction.

The good doctor's first prescription was a powerful opioid narcotic analgesic drug. Easing the pain, he believed, was the only way my belligerent eyelids would part. Though it upset my mother more than any other part of this saga, I took the prescription.

In the first few visits, I suffered the humilities of the doctor yelling at my eye to "Open! Open! Open! Damn it!" This was nothing compared to his habit of following me out the door with a bottle of disinfectant, spraying everything I came into contact with. I learned to walk as if I was about to be frisked.

When my eye finally opened for the fundus camera, the magnified photographs of my retina showed dozens of specks that looked like fish swirling in a pond.

"And that" —the doctor pointed to a black mark in a separate image— "is a scar on your cornea. Looks like a permanent one."

"Well, that's probably the pelican scar," I explained.

The good doctor seemed to think I was fibbing whenever I mentioned the dirty, rotten, smelly, no-good pelican that poked my eyeball.

He explained: "The eye is very fast to respond to damage, and is already healed from that scar. If the cause of your ailment was a pelican scratching your cornea, it would have become a bacterial infection. What we are dealing with is much worse. Much worse."

"How much worse?"

"Let me see. Before this, I treated the homeless in San Francisco. And out of four thousand patients," he clarified as dryly as a shedding iguana, "this is the worst case I've had to deal with." Blindness, he hinted, was a possibility I needed to prepare for.

Over the next few weeks of treatment, my eye would improve, deteriorate, improve, and deteriorate. The doctor was baffled, and he did not appear to believe my story.

My "pelican" became some kind of alibi according to the inevitable peanut gallery who were so quick to find fault in my tale. Colleagues were suspicious of the number of days I spent working from home or in complete darkness. One coworker pointed out, "the *first* time you told the story, the pelican's wingspan was THIS big, and *now* it's THIS BIG," as if anything I could simulate with my five-foot arm-span could exceed the wingspan of the saddest, runtiest pelican alive. Meanwhile, exaggeration in the retellings spiraled beyond my control. I began to hear my pelican debrief retold with a swashbuckling pelican as the hero. One account had justice delivered to me by the end of his beak—*ouch!* In another, the pelican retaliated after "some jerk-wad slapped it." I didn't even want to know what my mother thought of "the pelican" and its ability to get me prescription narcotics.

On the other end of the spectrum, responses varied from "That's nothing. I once got pecked by a *chicken!*" to "Pelicans are lame after you've been kicked by an ostrich."

Worst of all, I learned that the word "pelican" spontaneously incites people to recite Dixon Lanier Merritt's:

A wonderful bird is the pelican.
His bill can hold more than his belly can
He can hold in his beak
Enough food for a week,
But I'm damned if I see how the hell he can.

This poem, a veritable Goldfinger's industrial laser of verse to those of us who have lain on the pelican's cutting table, is etched in my head like a rosary prayer.

"I'm damned if I see how the hell I can *see*," I once told the doctor after he'd repeated the Limerick. He reacted by repositioning the fundus camera and shouting, "Now you know how *I* feel. *Wider!*" Humor, much like my face was becoming, was a very one-sided game in the office of Dr. Eyeball.

The good doctor and I had one thing in common: a love for travel. I'd been to New Zealand, he'd been to Australia, and we each wanted to visit the other land. Between sessions of "Wider! Wider! Wider!," we'd swap travel tips.

"And last time you were on the South Island," interrogated the good doctor, "did you see any moas?"

"No."

"No," he repeated without expression. "None flew over you?"

"No."

"Or kicked you?"

"No."

"Huh."

"I *did* get bucked and scratched by an ostrich once," I admitted.

"Have you ever considered maybe staying away from birds?"

No, I explained, large charismatic birds are what dreams are made of.

"I recommend small birds," he prescribed. "Finches don't kick."

The doctor's advice went unheeded, but he did manage to understand what was wrong with my eye. After weeks of experiment, he concluded that I had become allergic to the solution in certain brands of contact lenses. Even if I only wore a contact in my left eye for a day, it would affect my right eye for weeks. The fact that my glasses were broken in Belize was another problem altogether.

"Until we find a contact solution that you can *wing*, you'll have to drop the contacts cold *turkey*."

"Are you sure it had nothing to do with the pelican?" I asked. "It's too coincidental!"

"So far as I've learned from ophthalmology school," sighed Dr. Eyeball, "pelican isn't manufactured into *any* contact solution. Now, maybe the pelican had *something* to do with it. A voodoo curse, perhaps . . . You *did* deny him a fish."

In the end, we reached a compromise that the initial attack on my right eye—first by poison oak and then by pelican—had weakened it, making it more vulnerable to allergic reaction.

"Just as," he foreshadowed, "the allergic reaction has made your eye weaker still and prone to further infection."

Further infection by one thing or another continued for another month, and one after another experimental contact solution failed. Even if it wasn't his fault, I shook my fist at the photos of that pelican and cried, "It's because of you, dirty, rotten, smelly pelican!"

Shunning the light of day from my third-story apartment, I had to draw the curtains on the majestic valley oak outside. With one squinty eye, I could match hopping outlines through the backlit drapes with the chattering of oak titmice, the nagging *nyaaah nyaaah nyaaah nyaaah* of red-breasted nuthatches, and the trilling *prrrrrt prrrrrrt prrrrrrrrr* of Nuttall's woodpeckers. In the boughs of that oak, these passerines (and near-passerine) played out shadow puppet dramas worthy of the Globe Theatre. Titmouse antics are as mesmerizing in fast-motion as the pelican's in its slow, methodical dignity. The season turned and migrants appeared from the south. From my window, I heard some of the songbirds I'd met in Belize, and welcomed them.

Another month passed before my right eye took another turn for the worse, becoming bloodshot and scabby. I'd been to see Dr. Eyeball a few times before he decided it had to be, independently, the worst case of pink eye he had ever seen. "And no," he reassured me, "it's not the bird flu."

"Am I the worst patient you've ever had?"

"Telling you would be breaking the Hippocratic oath. But there was an angry pelican that came in once. Essential fatty-acids are important for your eyes," Dr. Eyeball explained, "but someone wouldn't let him eat any fish. . . "

Some jerk-wad, I assumed.

After another stretch under the good doctor's care, my pink eye was cured and we found a nonlethal contact solution. By the end of the fifth month, the fundus camera photographs no longer showed the swirling little fish. My Pelican Eye odyssey was over. Dr. Eyeball jumped with excitement and threw a fist in the air shouting, "I did it! I did it! I'm a genius!" I had never seen him break his deadpan, but I had to agree with his self-assessment.

"That pelican ought to see you now," said the doctor with triumph.

"So you finally believe me?" I asked with equal triumph.

"Of course," the doctor replied. "It's obvious that the pelican did a great deal of damage. I mean, look at all that scarring."

"You mean on my cornea?"

"I mean" —and he was as smooth as an ostrich claw in the ankle— "psychologically."

A year later, the good doctor's practice closed amid the recession. For all his joy in tormenting me with poetry, he was both a sympathetic and a generous man who charged me well under the premium. I've often wondered if his struggles curing my Pelican Eye helped in slowing down his business. That eye has since fallen victim to other terrors: the jungle, DEET, and web-toed salamander slime, to name a few. But with each trauma, I am reminded of Dr. Eyeball's parting advice: "If you ever get to Australia, stay away from Queensland. There are cassowaries. They kick."

My Pelican Eye may have been a *nomen dubium*, but I still credit that blue-banded pelican for helping reshape my outlook on birds. Nowadays, I'll spend hours trying to get glimpses of a new favorite—the wrentit—the enigmatic king within an elfin world called chaparral; or reveling in yellow-billed magpie melodrama. Lawrence's goldfinches have become an obsession to fill a void for the forgotten *Bathornis*. And a murmuration of tricolored blackbirds is as bewitching to me now as the homecoming pod of those so-called pterodactyls on our coast.

A wonderful bird is the pelican, whose creepy architecture has remained in vogue for thirty million years. Human history is a blink in the existence of the pelican, so when a pelican puts a five-month blink in the sight of one Quaternary whipper-snapper, I'll defer to its elder right. Considering all we've gotten away with during human-bird relations, I'll accept a reminder that in a world bereft of *Kelenken* or *Brontornis,* terror can still be a thing with feathers.

I regard the pelican more for the shiver that runs up my spine when I hear its graceful *whoosh* overhead. Perhaps that inexplicable nostalgia is rooted in the dread passed down from our *Australopithecine* ancestors from an age when death came from the sky. Or, maybe, it comes from an unfair association with an IBR pelican who deserved another chance. Maybe that pelican will find a way to exonerate himself of the blame, pain, and life lessons I hold him accountable for. And maybe he'll overcome his reputation and, someday, restore his good name. But I'm damned if I see how the hell he can.

ABOUT THE AUTHOR

IVAN PARR has worked in tour management, as a park naturalist, and as a consulting biologist. He does work in botany and wildlife, but is most interested in marine invertebrates, chaparral species, amphibians, and California endemics. In his spare time, he puts on workshops for the Western Section of The Wildlife Society, searches for obscure plants and animals, and enjoys nature photography. His photography website can be found here: www.californiabiodiversity.com.

TICKS, QUAILS, AND POLLYWOG TAILS—
THAT'S WHAT WILDLIFE BIOLOGISTS ARE MADE OF, OR SEVERAL HABITS OF A HIGHLY EFFECTIVE WILDLIFER

Matthew P. Bettelheim, CWB
Science Writer, Wildlife Research Biologist at AECOM,
and Natural Historian

1. Be prepared for family and clients alike to reduce your years of education, research, and experience in the field to "looking for critters."
2. Expect to be stopped by the police. Regularly. Contrary to what you might think, binoculars = Peeping Tom, roadside parking = drug deal, and any work involving rooftops (and, by extension, bridges) = jumper.
3. Billable hours are unforgiving. State and federal furloughs are unforgivable. Either way, expect to donate your time to get the job done right.
4. Standing in the middle of a marijuana field is not the time to practice your botany skills.

5. Whoever said, "Dress for the job you want, not the job you have" has clearly never worked in the field. When it comes to fieldwork, camouflage gives you invisibility, but a helmet and construction safety vest give you authority and safety. There is a time and a place for both—know the difference.

6. A state fish and game uniform automatically elevates you to "game warden" status. Study up on the question, "Where's a good place to hunt/fish?"

7. In Target, a uniform makes you a woodsman. In the woods, a uniform makes you a target. And in a field of marijuana, a uniform makes you an INS or border patrol agent.

8. Expect to drive a pickup if you work for a state or federal agency, a rental car if you work for a private consultant, and a desk if you stick around long enough.

9. Every phone call could lead to an invitation to survey lands never before explored with a naturalist's eyes. Savor those moments—they can be few and far between.

10. Remember that a good rancher knows their land as well as you know your way around a trusted field guide; the land is their livelihood, even if they don't know the Latin name of every grass and songbird. Take care you don't put more stock in a degree than you do in a lifetime of experience.
11. Still, take a landowner's wildlife sightings with a grain of salt. For every rancher who knows the difference between a coyote and a kit fox, there's one who thinks every crow is a California condor. Use your ears, but heed your head.

12. Permission-to-Enter means nothing when you are standing on the business end of a shotgun. On another man's land, the sword is mightier than the pen.
13. Learn to pee in the woods tactfully. Knowing the difference between someone keying out a bush and someone watering a bush will save you embarrassment down the road.
14. At the first mention of an endangered wildlife species during a construction tailboard meeting, odds are good the heavy machine operators and laborers alike will hijack the conversation to share with you their favorite golden eagle and California red-legged frog recipes. How you react will set the tone for the days ahead. Don't be a "bunny hugger"—offer them a recipe of your own to chew on.
15. Recognize that while your friends clock into their nine-to-five blue-chip and white-collar desk jobs, your office is the outdoors. You are getting paid to do what you did as a child: turn over rocks, count wildflowers, wade creeks, and watch wild animals. Count your blessings.

ABOUT THE AUTHOR

MATTHEW P. BETTELHEIM is a wildlife biologist, science writer, and natural historian whose writing portfolio includes feature articles in outlets like Bay Nature *magazine,* Berkeley Science Review, Inkling Magazine, Earth Island Journal, *and* Outdoor California. *He also manages and writes for* (bio)accumulation, *a regional blog that focuses on the natural world as it pertains to the history and natural history of the West Coast. In 2013, Matthew authored his first children's book,* Sardis and Stamm, *a story about the Antioch Dunes National Wildlife Refuge and the endangered Lange's metalmark butterfly. Matthew is a Certified Wildlife Biologist and has been a member of the Western Section of The Wildlife Society since 2003.*

YOU NEVER FORGET YOUR FIRST

Darren J. H. Sleep
Project Leader–Forest Ecology
National Council for Air and Stream Improvement, Inc.

They say you never forget your first.

I'm referring, of course, to owls.

Ever since I was a boy of six or seven, entranced by a swivel-headed barred owl in an aspen tree at my family's cottage, owls have captured my interest and imagination like no other creature. Whether I'm drawn to them because of their oversized, front-facing eyes, their eerie vocalizations, their silent flight, or their nocturnal habits, these birds of prey have since fueled my woodland wanderings and, to a large degree, my scientific inquisitiveness. I regret to this day that after I saw that first owl, I slept soundly that evening while the nesting pair went about their unseen business, keeping my parents awake most of the night with their ceaseless caterwauling, one of their more remarkable behaviors. I missed the entire show.

As I've pursued my career as a wildlife biologist, I have not always had the opportunity to work with owls, but I have gravitated when possible toward working with nocturnal wildlife while jumping at any opportunity to interact with these fascinating birds. My interactions with owls have been many over the years—sometimes hostile, which is often the case in encounters with breeding owls. I have been attacked, owing in no small part to bouts of thoughtlessness, meddling, or outright stupidity—by more than a half-dozen species of owl. I've been hit in the head by both northern saw-whets and boreal owls; wing-clapped by a long-eared owl; buzzed, dive-bombed, and screamed at by northern hawk owls; buzzed (and once bitten) by numerous great horned owls; and intimidated at dusk by a way-too-close great gray owl.

As a rule, breeding raptors are not fans of meddling biologists who play breeding calls next to established nests, or those who try to capture and band their young—even if temporarily—by smuggling them away from the nest tucked under a coat. Most of these encounters have been the result of a bird defending a territory or a mate, or protecting their young. Knowing this, it must be said I hold no grudge against owls. Most of these attacks were merely close calls, none resulted in injury (to either biologist or bird), and each interaction left me thrilling and marveling at these swooping, territorial birds.

But as long as I live, I will never forget my first interaction with a barred owl.

During my last year as an undergrad in Biology at the University of New Brunswick in Fredericton (Canada), I had an opportunity to undertake a senior research project and approached Dr. Tony Diamond, the biology department's resident ornithologist, about the opportunity to do a project on owls. To be clear, I was explicit that I was not interested in simply writing a report; I wanted to do something with real, live owls. My enthusiasm was enough that he paired me with a PhD student by the name of Peter McKinley, who was working on a passerine study in central New Brunswick. I have no idea what arm-twisting or blackmail behind closed doors was required, but Peter agreed to take me into the field and give me some pointers on surveying for owls. Whatever the terms of the agreement, in hindsight I'm convinced to this day that Peter got a bad deal.

It was mid-March, and although fairly cold, New Brunswick had experienced some early thaws that year. The snow was deep in places, and many of the forest roads had soft, muddy areas. Through active forest management, most of the roads were kept open throughout the year, but no one was operating in our particular area at the time, so we had a vast landscape to ourselves. The study site was a couple of hours' drive from Fredericton in central New Brunswick. The roads twisted into the Acadian forest, where maples, beech, poplar, and balsam firs populated the rolling hills and occasional steep ravines. It was a veritable haven for forest-dwelling creatures.

After some discussion, Peter and I had settled on a protocol to follow for our owl surveys. At the time, playback surveys using tape recordings of owl calls were a known but uncommon practice. Owls—especially breeding pairs—are territorial, and will respond to calls made by foreign owls with calls of their own. On occasion, they'll even approach the unknown caller to investigate and, if necessary, protect their territory.

We decided to use a battery-powered twin-speaker tape deck to play some recordings I had pulled from an Audubon collection. The protocol consisted of driving down the forest access roads, stopping at set intervals to broadcast in succession first the call of the great horned owl twice, then the barred owl twice, and lastly the saw-whet owl twice, each separated by one minute of silence as a listening interval between each call. Before nightfall, we drove the route and identified and flagged each listening station with the idea that, later that evening, we would return and record any owl species (and the direction of their calls) that responded during the playback sessions at each location.

As we were flagging the eighth or ninth listening station, we discovered—much to our delight—a barred owl perched alongside the road. When we drove off, he flew ahead of us down the road, eventually veering off into the dense forest. In hindsight, we should have recognized that seeing an owl so easily before dusk was an indication of something, but we paid it no heed.

As we kicked off our survey that evening, we were initially met with few responses. We were probably late in the breeding season; as a result, it was likely that many of the pairs already had well-established nests, and the "hens" (as female owls are known) were sitting on eggs and unlikely to respond. Each and every time we heard a distant call, my ears perked up. We heard a couple of saw-whets, a distant barred owl, and one great horned owl.

When we arrived at the listening station where we had seen the barred owl near the road, he was nowhere to be seen, but by now it was well past dusk. As per our protocol, we placed the tape deck on the roof of the truck and hit play. The clear and loud tone of the great horned owl's *Who's-awake . . . meeee tooo . . .* rang out loud and clear.

I will never forget the response.

Just out of eyesight, somewhere in the woods not far from where we stood, came the most spine-tingling noise I have ever heard in my life. Anyone who has ever heard the aggressive territorial call of a barred owl knows what I'm talking about. It's less a gentle *Hoot* and more a terrifying raptorial scream.

"Uh . . . Pete? What was that?" I asked.

The sound came again, but louder this time, closer, more intimidating.

"I dunno . . ." Peter replied. "BUT HERE IT COMES!"

At the edge of my vision came two eyes out of the darkness flanked by outstretched wings, at chest-height. I had no idea what sort of winged devilry was barreling toward me, nor had I any idea what to do about it. Fortunately, my legs recognized the threat to my upper body that my brain couldn't and—understanding that their survival depended on the rest of me—they simply collapsed, allowing my weight to carry me to the wet, muddy ground.

An owl passed over me, two to three feet above the ground, and alighted in a nearby tree where he was became visible in the headlights of the truck. I stood up, neglecting for the moment my now-mud-encrusted attire, and instead marveled at the barred owl in the tree. He sat there, his black eyes revealing no malice. His head swiveling effortlessly back and forth, sweeping his piercing gaze into the darkness to either side of him so nonchalantly, he might as well have been waiting for the 10:05 Acadian Evening Express bus to arrive at any moment. In contrast, my eyes were as big as dinner plates, and my heart was

thumping audibly in my chest as I was intoxicated by a mixture of excitement, shock, and primal fear.

I was just preparing to compose myself—perhaps try for a picture—when the one-minute listening interval ran its course and the barred owl call rang out from the tape deck with an enthusiastic *Who-cooks-for you. . .* The owl instantly spread his wings and dove from his perch, his eyes fixed on me.

As my brain registered a muddled, "What the . . . ," my legs responded with "Drop him," and once again I found myself face-first in the muck.

I recovered quickly, grabbing the stereo as Pete and I ducked into the truck. And there, in the cab of the pickup, we were treated to one of the most amazing spectacles of the north woods as the female joined the male across the clearing and the pair launched into a full-spectrum barred owl duet.

For those who have never heard a pair of barred owls in full duet, it never fails to amaze. Launching into a cacophony aptly compared by others to the sound of howler monkeys, or described as "caterwauling," the pair perch near each other and together make such incredibly loud and terrifying vocalizations so unworldly, it is difficult to imagine them coming from a creature like an owl. The pair can carry on for hours, bobbing and weaving their heads up and down together.

I was completely and utterly thunderstruck. As we moved on to the next survey point, I forgot that I was covered in mud and began recounting our encounter with the owls nonstop, no doubt giving those barred owls in our taillights a run for their money. I had never seen or heard anything so amazing in my life, I said in a thousand different ways, and this was only my first foray into fieldwork!

Peter was extremely good-natured about it, enough to let my enthusiasm and my mouth run unchecked for the next few hours. To his credit, he was working on his PhD in songbird ecology at the time, and more accustomed to waking early rather than staying up late. By the time 4:00 a.m. rolled around, and we were ready to pack it in, he was clearly exhausted—while my excitement had hardly ebbed. At that point, I recall him looking over at me and simply asking me in no uncertain terms to, "Please shut the #&@$ up." I did my level best to take the message in stride, and contained my enthusiasm until the next morning.

That encounter (with the barred owls, not with tired Peter) stuck with me and became the catalyst for my later career as a wildlife biologist. It's true that field biology can be at times dull, tiring, or uncomfortable, but it is the possibility of a chance encounter like mine, to catch a glimpse of rare and unusual animals and the opportunity to learn about them, that has kept me in this profession for over two decades and, if I'm lucky, for years to come.

ABOUT THE AUTHOR

DARREN J. H. SLEEP is Project Leader—Forest Ecology, with the National Council for Air and Stream Improvement (NCASI), based in Montreal, Quebec. He is responsible for a national-level research program encompassing projects that are of interest to the forest products manufacturing sector. His work covers such broad topics as wildlife and biodiversity, watershed management, and conservation planning. His primary research interests focus on the assessment and management of rare and endangered species, and the relationships between species and their habitats. He has served in a science advisory role with the Canadian Boreal Forest

Agreement and has been an active member of The Wildlife Society since 2004. Darren is a Certified Wildlife Biologist and was a founding member of the Canadian Section of The Wildlife Society (2007), and served in several executive positions, including as President of the Section from 2014—2015. He is sometimes found just outside of Montreal, Quebec, where his family insists they've seen him recently.

KICK IT IN THE ICE HOLE

Dr. Charles "Chuck" Jonkel
(July 16, 1930–April 12, 2016)
Co-Founder & President Emeritus, Great Bear Foundation

The night he scared himself, he sent his friend Henk Kiliaan home after all their reminiscing. Scaring himself wasn't hard to do—what with the whiteouts and the polar bears (always the polar bears), helicopters falling from the sky, and the vast whiteness of it all and everything in between. Lost in the high Arctic, where he couldn't have been more alone no matter the company he kept. He might have done stupid things in his youth. Hell, he *had* done stupid things in adulthood, too. But he had also lived a full life, all in the name of science, that truly began in the high Arctic when he set out to answer a simple question: How *do* you catch a polar bear?

To answer that question, Dr. Charles "Chuck" Jonkel joined the Canadian Wildlife Service in 1966. His assignment, in short, was to find out where the polar bears were.

In the years to follow, it would become one of life's many ironies: for all the time Jonkel spent working with polar bears, he never sought out bear work. "I wasn't really looking for bears. The bears found me," he explained. When polar bears found him in 1966, Jonkel quickly filled a much-needed niche, becoming the first polar bear biologist in the Canadian Wildlife Service; the first scientist to perform a systematic, non-anecdotal study of polar bears; and thus the founder and pioneer of polar bear biology.

Born in Chicago during the Depression, Charles; his brother, George—who was two years Charles's senior; and their older sister, Theo, were raised by their single mother, Ruby. When Charles was "a little pike" of two years old, Ruby picked up and moved the Jonkel children to northern Wisconsin. They were raised for a time by their grandparents on the family farm while Ruby worked odd jobs. At age five, Charles roamed the woods with George and a .22, hunting squirrel and poaching deer for red meat. At night, they switched to hunting raccoon and skunk, making up for lost sleep in school the next day.

When Charles was seven, the Jonkel children moved to another farm. After the boys finished their farm chores, a neighbor taught Charles how to trap mink and muskrat. Ever resourceful, Charles was soon working his own trapline and the boys would skin the carcasses, prepare the pelts, and sell the meat to the local fish and game hunting club for fifty cents a pound. The boys knew they were operating outside the law—they knew about game wardens, and thought there were wardens "hidden behind every bush and every tree." But the wardens knew nothing of the Jonkel boys and left them be.

Unbeknownst to Charles or George, as they became young men and left the farm and the woods behind to pursue higher education, they were not putting away childish things. Rather, throughout their childhood, they had inadvertently learned the fundamentals of a bourgeoning profession that had yet to be born, but for which they were both destined—that of the wildlife biologist.

"I got very interested in wildlife that way, and so did my brother," Jonkel explained, thinking back on his boyhood.

"Little by little we did more hunting and such, and then [George] found out that you could actually go to school and work with wildlife—learn about wildlife and get jobs."

"There were agencies who were starting by that time to hire wildlife biologists. A lot of people really didn't think [biologists] were scientists or researchers," said Jonkel. They thought biologists were just playing with wildlife. "But you know, gradually, it became a profession and both of us stayed in it."

George gravitated toward birds, starting off with the Montana Fish and Game Department and working his way toward Chief of the Bird Banding Laboratory in the Office of Migratory Bird Management with the U.S. Fish and Wildlife Service. Charles gravitated toward mammals. And it was a good thing he did, because, as Jonkel reasoned, "Bears kept falling in my lap."

In 1957, during his last week at the University of Montana, Jonkel was invited to join a pine marten study as a Master's student. Minus the bears—who had been forever ruining his pine marten traps, smashing them to steal the bait—that work went well enough. But as he was wrapping up that study in 1959, Jonkel—just married and a new father—found himself at a crossroads with just two job offers: rake leaves on campus, or start a black bear study. Except for the untold hours spent cursing them during his pine marten study, he knew nothing about bears. But even though "the leaf job paid better," Jonkel set off to study black bears in Montana's Whitefish Range.

In the years to come, Jonkel kept returning to bears: pine marten, black bear, moose, black bear. Even when he was working on moose, he used the moose as a cover for his affairs with bears. "I'd pretend I was going out to work on moose, but in fact I'd go out and sneak around doing some more work on the black bears."

Perhaps it was kismet when, just as Jonkel was finishing his PhD on black bears in 1966, a biologist with the Canadian Wildlife Service walked into his office and said, "We want to start a polar bear study. We heard you know how to work on bears." He did, and he needed that job. There was just one thing: he knew little about polar bears and even less about the Arctic. But inexperience hadn't stopped him before.

Up until Jonkel first set foot in the Arctic, most of what was known about polar bears had been gleaned from the anecdotal accounts of early European explorers or from captive bears in zoos. On three occasions, zookeepers took Jonkel aside to warn him, "Son, those polar bears will hunt you all the time." That was the behavior the keepers witnessed of polar bears in captivity. Polar bears on display would stalk zoo staff with their characteristic creep across the ice—belly to the ground; head and haunches low; forelimbs dragging at their sides; inching along, propelled by the push of their rear toenails digging into the ice like crampons. Jonkel would come to learn that this instinctual behavior was simply how polar bears crept up on their prey, to get close enough to ringed seals undetected, to run and strike before the seals escaped down a hole in the ice. It was a matter of survival; they were practicing, and it was nothing personal.

To the contrary, in the years that followed, Jonkel would come to know polar bears as more curious than anything else, like big pussycats compared to the grizzlies and black bears on which he cut his teeth. At least, as long as you weren't a ringed seal (or, he later reasoned, wrapped up in a sleeping bag on the ice such that you might be *mistaken* for a ringed seal). But that didn't mean the danger he and other researchers faced in the Arctic wasn't real or constant. It was both.

The early days of bear research were ones of trial and error. Before the advent of immobilization drugs, for researchers to handle wild animals required—as one journal article put it—"gloves, rope, and intestinal fortitude."

"Before [the dart gun]," Jonkel said, "you couldn't do research on bears because there was no way to handle them. With deer, antelope, grouse, and squirrels and such, you could just wrestle them down, or find them in a fox trap, and squeeze them, and tag them, and tattoo them. But with bears you couldn't do that sort of thing."

When the dart gun first became commercially available after 1958, they *could* do that sort of thing. And biologists did. In 1959, the same year Jonkel began working with Montana's black bears, three other bear studies kicked off that would pioneer new ground. The Craigheads with Yellowstone's grizzlies. Art Pearson's Yukon grizzlies. And Douglas Pierson's black bears on the Olympic peninsula in Washington State.

Although bear biology was ramping up, the science of immobilization drugs was still in its infancy. The early drugs available at that time had been developed for people or veterinary uses, and rarely if ever tested on wildlife. In much the same way human and veterinary medicine differ, administering a drug properly to a bear requires insight into dose and schedule—how much and how frequently—which can vary between wildlife species.

For that reason, there were no clinical drug trials or dosing guidelines for a 400- to 1,400-pound bear—and certainly no guidelines for polar bears. That service was performed in the field on an if-needed, as-needed basis by researchers like Jonkel.

With the great outdoors as their laboratory, for each new bear species, researchers had to learn how to physically *handle* them—how to immobilize them, how to tag them, and how to track them—relatively simple things today that fall within any contemporary bear biologist's wheelhouse. But with each new bear study, Jonkel and his cohorts were inventing the wheel.

So when Jonkel switched gears to tackle polar bears, he was starting with a clean slate.

One of the earliest drugs available to researchers was Sucostrin (Succinylcholine chloride). Although Sucostrin was cheap and fast-acting and relatively safe for the researcher, it was only a muscle blocking-agent; it paralyzed an animal, but it left them fully awake, aware, and capable of feeling pain and stress. And like any chemical agent, tolerance levels varied between species, and no one before Jonkel had tried it on a polar bear. After losing their first polar bear to an overdose, Jonkel erred on the side of caution. Rather than giving multiple doses, he would instead feel out the bear's state of mind. "If we were almost done, we'd just hold the animal, pin him down, and hold him until we'd get the last measurements taken, and then we'd clear the area—literally hold them down and jump up and run. Hope they didn't come after us."

Sometimes, the bear would just stand up and walk away—the textbook definition of a close call. Gaston Tessier, a wildlife biologist with the Canadian Wildlife Service, wasn't the only one to recall an instance when Jonkel instructed him to sit on a bear's neck as he finished tagging the bear's ears. "He says, 'You just sit on the neck,'" Tessier recalled. "I mean, the bear just lifted up and [I] went tumbling and that was it. There was no way we could keep him down."

One of Jonkel's early litmus tests was to stick his boot in the bear's mouth, judging its expected recovery by the strength of the bear's jaw and, in turn, when it was time to leave. At least once, his technicians remember, when Jonkel gave the bear the boot, the bear bit back harder than Jonkel cared for.

But there was never ill will between Jonkel and his bears. "I had a few chase me, but most of the time they were just kind of like, *What did you do that for?* They'd look at the dart, look at you, and ask, *How come you hurt me?*"

Once Jonkel's crew had confirmed the bear was sedated, they had fifteen minutes—eighteen minutes at best—to collect a blood sample, remove a premolar, measure (or estimate) weight, and take body measurements. Bears also received a unique tattoo and an ear tag for identification purposes. Early on, Jonkel himself cheerfully lugged a clunky tripod contraption across the tundra that allowed them to suspend a bear in a net long enough to weigh it. From the data he collected, Jonkel soon learned that a height and width (girth) measurement were all he needed to estimate a rough weight, and with that knowledge he became adept at eyeballing body weights and doses.

In the years to come, walking surveys were augmented by the addition of helicopters and small fixed-wing aircraft to track polar bears, locate dens, and cover more ground.

The researchers also learned how to tranquilize a bear while in the air from the cockpit of a helicopter, but not before they learned how to estimate weight to make sure the dose met the Goldilocks standard. With experience, Jonkel mastered that, too, allowing them to track and tranquilize bears from a safe distance before landing to collect the necessary data.

Nevertheless, there were times—too many to count—when Jonkel's team would have to perform artificial respiration on a thousand-plus-pound bear. You could say Jonkel wrote the book on polar bear CPR, a not-so-delicate maneuver that consisted of him grabbing a fistful of skin near the bear's rib cage and another by the shoulder, and then tugging on them like a stuck drawer. Using his knee and all his body weight, Jonkel would force the air from the bear's lungs with each downward thrust, resulting in a sucking sound when the rib cage expanded as he let off his weight and tugged at the bear's chest, like someone loosening the stays on a bearskin corset.

Reviving a bear could take as long as half an hour of kneading its chest like abalone meat—no small feat in the Arctic. But

Jonkel liked bears. To Jonkel, losing a bear was more like losing a personal friend.

One of the ways to catch a polar bear was to trap them. For this, Jonkel devised a makeshift lean-to of driftwood and rocks, within which he placed a foot snare baited with kippers or sardines. Each snare was anchored in place with a fifty-gallon barrel filled with sand and rocks for drag. When they caught bears, more often than not they found that after a brief struggle with the weighted barrel, the individuals would just lie down stoically. It was rare for them to respond with aggression or violence: rather, more of an Eeyore ho-hum resignation. One bear became infamous for using the traps as a tapas bar, learning that the researchers would set him free after each appetizer.

During their first year, Jonkel and his team ran miles of traplines to identify polar bear hubs where activity was greatest. The traps were set a mile apart, requiring fifteen to twenty miles of walking to check every trap. And once set, every trap had to be checked daily, no matter the weather—to leave one unattended ran the risk of a bear losing a limb or succumbing to the elements.

During one foray into the Arctic with field technician and photographer Fred Bruemmer, the pair came across a bear caught in one of their foot snares. Before they set to work, Jonkel darted it. Jonkel knew that as a rule, polar bears didn't get alarmed even in situations like this. "If you weren't a ringed seal, you weren't important to the bear." And anyhow, this bear appeared quite tractable, despite the befuddled look the bear was giving the dart in his chest. With a glance at Jonkel, as if to ask the polar bear mantra, *What'd you do that for?* the bear put his head down in his paws. Worried that the bear wasn't "under" enough, he instructed Bruemmer to distract the bear while he moved in close behind and stuck the bear in the leg with a hand syringe. Again, the bear looked over his shoulder

at Jonkel with another *What'd you do that for?* before he succumbed to sleep. It was only after they had finished working up
the bear that Jonkel went to retrieve the first dart and learned
that it hadn't discharged—he had administered the second
dose to a 700-pound polar bear that was as sober as a judge.

Mishaps like that weren't uncommon, either. After running
a trapline in Churchill with his first field technician, Henk
Kiliaan, they retraced their footsteps at the end of a day in the
field to check on a bear they had sedated earlier to make sure it
had sobered up. Night was falling fast, so they were left to use
the headlights of their pickup truck to find the bear.

When the supine bulk of a bear huddled on the ground
appeared in the headlights, Jonkel was quick to jump out of
the cab as he said, "Stop, there she is." Running up to the
recumbent bear, he booted it firmly under the tail, right up
the rear end, to jar it from any drug haze. In response, the bear
reared up in surprise, sprung to all fours, and—with a glance at
Jonkel—"got the hell out of town."

Meanwhile, from the safety of the truck cab, Kiliaan had
noticed that the bear in the headlights getting the boot had
no numbers spray-painted on its side as an identifying mark.
It wasn't their bear. Sure enough, several minutes later, they
found *their* bear, still recuperating from the tranquilizer, fifteen
to twenty yards away. "He booted the wrong bear up the bun-
nies!" recalled Kiliaan with laughter.

In another instance, Jonkel was working a bear with a
trapping assistant when the need arose to roll the bear over
onto its stomach to make sure it could breathe coming out
of the drug. As the assistant dug in to roll the bear's hindquarters, he noticed Jonkel struggling with the front end. At
first, he thought Jonkel, whose arm had found its way into
the bear's open mouth, was pantomiming a scene out of *The
Pink Panther*, swatting the bear across the nose like Inspector

Clouseau fending off the relentless advances of Cato. Except it was no joke. The bear had awoken enough to quite literally bear down on Jonkel's exposed arm, a pair of canines piercing his wrist bones. By sheer luck, Jonkel was saved by his parka, which had become bunched up between the bear's molars. In the years to follow, he showed off the white scars on his wrist with pride at cocktail parties.

But some scars weren't appropriate for the cocktail party rotation. One Friday, technician Frank Brazeau was invited along on a trip to Somerset Island with Jonkel and Tessier to assist with polar bear tagging. Jonkel—who at that time was interested in collecting data on the dimensions and construction of dens—wanted to explore some lakes he had found on a map. On the lakes, he reasoned, they'd find snowdrifts, and snowdrifts were prime bear maternity den habitat.

Upon their arrival, Jonkel read the lay of the land before they touched the helicopter down a distance uphill of a snowdrift that contained a den within its powdery bowels. Jonkel—who knew from experience that the typical den began at the toe of a drift and climbed upward, a polar bear stratagem to conserve heat—led the way downhill, circling the concealed den on their approach to avoid trampling it. At the den entrance, Jonkel left Brazeau outside to take notes and, dropping on all fours, wriggled his way in and up thirty or forty feet of tunnel. It wasn't until he hit a bend in the tunnel, however, that Jonkel realized he was in over his head and, growing uncomfortable with the situation, began backing down the tunnel to regroup and rethink their situation.

Meanwhile, from where he had been standing guard outside, Brazeau had developed a hankering for a cigarette and, upon seeing Jonkel's hindquarters wriggling back the way they had come, made a beeline for the helicopter. By the time Jonkel had worked his shoulders and then his head free of the den's maw, it was too late for him to call Brazeau back, much less explain why they had circled the drift in the first place.

As Brazeau was climbing the drift on his way back to the helicopter, he had unknowingly walked across the bear's ceiling and, backlit by the sun overhead, had announced himself by casting a shadow through the thin ten inches of snow. Before Jonkel could cry out, Brazeau felt a sinking sensation, like the snow was folding up beneath his feet. Seconds later, a head and then two yellow paws emerged from the snow like a hirsute Lady of the Lake to sink her teeth into his leg. As Brazeau dropped, surprised, into the den six or seven feet, he went down swinging, throwing punches and shouting for all he was worth.

"Down the hole I went, and I got up and I start swinging. I seen fur and went for it. I seen the bear face-to-face, and I start swinging and swinging," Brazeau remembers.

Between punches, Brazeau recalls the sow recoiling at his antics, as though she was quickly reconsidering her hasty invitation, and that there were three cubs in the den with them.

Jonkel, meanwhile, had leaped into action when he heard Brazeau shout, "Help! She's got me!" Clambering up the drift to where he had last seen Brazeau, he was met with an outstretched pair of parka-clad arms when he peered into the six-foot hole. Between Jonkel and Brazeau, it is unclear to this day whether Jonkel pulled Brazeau to freedom or the bear threw Brazeau back.

By the time the sow had composed herself enough to pop out of her den's new skylight, her two massive paws outstretched in the snow, framing her emerging head like bookends, Jonkel and Brazeau had run like hell for the helicopter. On their way back to Resolute Bay, Jonkel and Tessier radioed ahead for the hospital to expect them. As the nurses debated whether to give Brazeau a tetanus shot, Jonkel interceded: "Oh, don't give him anything. Think of that poor bear. Who's going to give *her* the rabies shot?"

Because of the groundwork laid by Jonkel to mark, track, and collect data on individual bears—laid in many instances on hands and knees in a polar bear's den—we have a better understanding today of polar bear natural history. As we now know, polar bears have a circumpolar range that encompasses landmasses and icepacks within the Arctic Circle in Greenland, Norway, Russia, the United States (Alaska), and Canada. Because they spend so many months of the year at sea, they are considered marine mammals. While they typically move at a leisurely speed of three miles an hour, they can travel thirty-one miles in a twenty-four-hour period, and swim at speeds of up to six miles an hour for up to forty miles, all within home ranges that can approach 230,000 square miles.

Excluding the southernmost Canadian polar bears that reside in Hudson Bay, who follow the sea ice north, most populations are centered around the Arctic ice pack and follow the sea ice south as it grows in winter, and then retreat northward in summer as it recedes, traveling between ice floes in search of food. With climate change, the ice sheets polar bears rely on to travel and hunt are increasingly disappearing, leaving them stranded or forcing them to swim longer distances than usual, threatening these bears' hard-earned way of life.

Polar bears subsist primarily on ringed seals, but also bearded, hooded, and harp seals, as well as the occasional walrus, reindeer, and beluga whale. Those polar bears in the southern range that spend more time on land become omnivorous, and will eat anything from bird eggs and tundra fruits to small mammals, geese and gulls, char and sculpin, and in an unfortunate turn, human garbage from bins and landfills.

Dens are constructed in snowdrifts (in the north) or snow and earth chambers (in the south) for shelter from the elements, temperature regulation, protection from insects and other bears, or to rear young. Maternity dens are often carefully designed and constructed with entrance tunnels and various chambers that plunge below the snowline into the permafrost or earth below.

In their search for dens like these, Jonkel learned to take to the skies in March and April to scour the shorelines for the tracks of newly emerged sows and their cubs traveling between their inland dens and the sea ice. Up until then, terrestrial denning areas had been needles in a haystack. But they soon learned that fresh paw prints were like bread crumbs they could backtrack straight to maternity dens. There, in a feat of fearlessness that didn't come in Crackerjack boxes, Jonkel would crawl inside—like he had attempted that fateful day Brazeau got a firsthand look at a polar bear den—and take measurements of the polar bears' wintery hobbit holes.

As Jonkel would come to learn, life on the ice wasn't easy if you were anything other than a polar bear. Traveling by sled dogs, Ski-Doo snowmobiles, canoes, Peterhead and longline fishing boats, Jet Ranger bush helicopters, small twin-engine planes, or by foot if necessary, Jonkel and his team would work fifteen- to eighteen-hour days, seven days a week, without regard for day or night, then return for a large meal, assemble their gear, eat a second dinner, and then do it all again. Sometime in there they would find time to sleep—often throwing down their Black's-brand Icelandic down sleeping bags in an igloo or a tent or a plywood shanty or a heated storehouse when a hotel or motel wasn't available. But always they were on the clock in the daily struggle to survive the Arctic.

At night, it wasn't uncommon for polar bears to visit Jonkel's team as they slept. As a rule, they never stowed their rifles in an igloo—condensation from their breath or body heat might form in the barrel of the rifle and freeze in the cold, running the risk of the barrel exploding if they had to fire it. The solution was to stow their rifle just outside in a gun case and scratch the outline of the gun into the inside of the igloo so that, if the need arose, they could cut through the wall with a snow knife in an emergency to reach the gun.

Temporary igloos, such as those built to support transient researchers, had a shelf life of two to three days, which was ample for one-nighters, or three if they were waiting for the weather to break or a lift back to civilization. Sometimes when they doubled back, they would find their igloos collapsed, surrounded by signs that a curious polar bear had clambered on top to investigate.

Out in the boonies, a meal was often what was at hand. Caribou carcasses were skinned and draped across the komatik, the traditional Inuit sled. Anyone who grew hungry could chop off a chunk of meat and eat it like frozen candy. Caribou they ate raw, and ptarmigan they ate fresh, warm, and raw. And when they were in the company of the local Inuit, sometimes there was walrus liver or char.

Once, one of Jonkel's assistants recalls, they discovered their oatmeal had been tainted with gasoline. They ate it anyway. "I can still remember what it's like after breakfast to burp and taste gasoline," he said.

On Northern Coats Island in 1967, the researchers stumbled into a food cache left behind by a C.R. Anderson of the Geological Survey of Canada. Jonkel's food stores had run low, so the men gave little thought to the four-to-five-year-old-cans' missing labels and rust and devoured the fruit cocktail and peaches.

But Jonkel was himself renowned for even more curious eating habits. He once pulled a piece of barbeque chicken out of his pocket and offered it to a colleague who had forgotten his lunch, and was known for leaving Styrofoam cups in the refrigerator that were unidentifiable due to the rime of congealed fat that perched near the rim like an Arctic espresso.

Tracking polar bears from a helicopter, it was easy to get caught up in the moment, finding themselves two to three hundred miles between where they had filed their position for the day and where the bears led them. Even then, they still found time to instruct the pilot to double back so they could snap a photograph, or set down for a picnic or coffee break or to sneak in some fishing.

Between the pileups and flameouts and crashes, they had to invent ways to keep the helicopters in service, to deal with unexpected storms, to find fuel caches. Sometimes, the real challenge was simply being able to take care of yourself, especially when nobody else knew where they were. "It was you and the polar bears and the ice and the snow and the helicopter and the pilot. And that was it." And sometime things simply went south.

During one memorable 1972 trip between islands in the Canadian High Arctic, on a flight from the weather station at

Eureka to Resolute Bay, Jonkel and Kiliaan found themselves in a whiteout so absolute, not even their pilot, Gene Vernet, knew left from right, much less up from down. It was like they were inside of a Ping-Pong ball, Jonkel said.

At Jonkel's suggestion, the pilot hugged the coast, zigzagging between thin spots in the cloudbank. Even that wasn't enough to keep them on course. Jonkel remembers looking down in time to see rocks racing toward his feet before the helicopter skipped once, twice, between what could only be the ground before skidding into a snowdrift and tipping over on its side.

In the silence that followed, the three men hung suspended by their seat belts.

Jonkel, who was closest to the ground when the helicopter came to rest, began struggling to free himself from the wreckage. Instead, his kicking and flailing legs only served to jiggle the cockpit up and down like a seesaw, held in place and strapped to his seat as he was by his safety belt.

Realizing their predicament, Kiliaan yelled, "Take your Goddam seat belt off!" while Vernet yelled, "She's gonna blow, she's gonna blow!"

Jonkel unstrapped himself and—the others following suit—tumbled onto the tundra and clear of the crash. But it didn't blow. Once they could assess the situation, it became apparent that the cockpit bubble they had escaped from—the helicopter's all-glass canopy—was cracked but intact. But the radio was out of commission, the emergency survival beacon wasn't working, and the battery was dead. They were all alone with no one to hear them but the polar bears.

Stranded, they had little recourse but to make the best of their situation. After pitching a pup tent recovered from the helicopter, they salvaged the pilot seats—that hours before they had feared might be their marble slabs—and fashioned them into makeshift field cots. Kiliaan's attempts to sneak up polar bear–like on a seal with his rifle were unsuccessful, so they snacked on spare food from their bags.

Lady Luck smiled on them hours later when they were awoken around midnight by the *whup-whup-whup* of an approaching helicopter. Like the three polar castaways, the pilots of this second helicopter had also been feeling their way blind through the whiteout. Nursing their coffees, the pilots mistook the three men running from their tents barefoot in fifteen- to twenty-below-freezing for Inuit before they noticed the stranded chopper and the smoke from Kiliaan's hastily deployed emergency flare, set down, and brought the three back safely to the Polar Continental Shelf Program facility in Resolute Bay.

* * *

When Charles Jonkel left the high Arctic two years later in 1974, he returned to Montana to continue studying black bears. There in Missoula, he realized his passion and activism for protecting bears by cofounding the Great Bear Foundation in 1981, the nonprofit bear conservation organization "dedicated to the conservation of the eight species of bears and their habitat around the world," including the polar bear. Jonkel served as foundation President Emeritus and Scientific Advisor until he passed away in Missoula, Montana, on April 12, 2016, at the age of eighty-five. Jonkel devoted more than fifty years to bear biology, conservation, and education, during which time he co-drafted the International Agreement on the Conservation of Polar Bears (the first ever international agreement to protect and conserve polar bear populations) and founded the International Wildlife Film Festival. With any luck—and luck had certainly been on his side over the years—Charles Jonkel's wish of being reincarnated as a polar bear on North Twin Island has been granted.

ABOUT THE AUTHOR

This account of **DR. CHARLES JONKEL** *'s work with polar bears was written by Matthew Bettelheim and is based heavily on the oral histories collected by the Great Bear Foundation about polar bear pioneer Charles Jonkel and his life. Of particular importance was foundation executive director Shannon Donahue's thesis "The Last Standing Bear: A Documentary Film on the Life and Work of Charles Jonkel." Since 2008, Shannon has been collaborating with Frank Tyro and Matt Anderson to bring their documentary celebrating Jonkel to the big screen. The film has since been released at the 2017 International Wildlife Film Festival under the title,* Walking Bear Comes Home: The Life and Work of Chuck Jonkel, *and is available at the Great Bear Foundation website,* www.greatbear.org.

LOST AND FOUND

J. Drew Lanham, PhD, CWB

Alumni Distinguished Professor and Master Teacher
Clemson University Department of Forestry
and Environmental Conservation

For almost as long as I've been alive, I've been a birder. No, my parturition (birth date for you non-wildlings) didn't come complete with a tiny pair of bins slung around my infantile neck, but not too long after, my entry birds became a big part of who I would become. With a self-certified start in the second grade and a portly spectacled gray-haired teacher, Ms. Beasley, who cultivated my already burgeoning avian-oriented, nature-loving propensities, it didn't take much beyond the mimeographed outlines of a mockingbird to convince her and others that I was either a very odd child, an ornithologist in the making, or both. You see, as other eight-year-olds were coloring their very own *Mimus polyglottus* all sorts of obscenely assorted (and scientifically incorrect) colors, I was carefully shading my mimeographed mimic thrush with my big thick second-grader pencil in carefully crafted tones of black and gray.

Unimaginative? Yes. Ornithologically accurate? Yes.

An ornithologist-birder was fledged.

From my earliest nurturing in my backwoods upbringing in Edgefield, South Carolina—a place where wild turkeys always seemed abundant and white-tailed deer never read the early 1970s news of their demise, I've been more interested in being outside than in. My parents were science teachers. Mama taught biology and Daddy earth sciences. The crucible of the family farm ensconced in the midst of the Long Cane Ranger District of the Sumter National Forest perhaps meant that an early genetic and environmental die was cast. The hardening for that rural nature-nurture destiny then came with my first field guide and constant (but unsuccessful) attempts to fly without the aid of machines already proven in the task. By the time I was ten, I'd launched myself from ladders, rooftops, haystacks, and trees with cardboard wings, plastic garbage bag parachutes, and umbrellas in attempts to be one of the birds I watched. Somehow gravity always won. The Golden Guide I'd finally saved enough quarters to buy was my entry into another world where I didn't have to fly; the birds did it for me. I could look at the range maps of things I saw in the fields and woods—song sparrows or summer tanagers—and know that the places they flew to were far away from the place I lived.

I read field guides, tirelessly studied the "B" volume of the old Compton's Encyclopedia, and cached the idea of bird study in my brain as what I wanted to do for the rest of my life.

Unfortunately, the folks responsible for guiding high school students through the maze of prospective careers saw things differently. As a black kid who did okay in math and science, I was advised that any decision in the direction of a college major like wildlife biology or, heaven forbid, zoology, would dead-end me in a career as a forest ranger or zookeeper. Besides, black people didn't do such things. Why not do something respectable, acceptable, and lucrative instead? And if I wanted to keep up this wildlife thing, then I'd have the money as an

engineer to follow my passions part-time as a hobby. Trapped by this advisement and the almost automatic decision to push any kid of color into some engineering pigeonhole, I was off to college with the other hordes of black engineers-to-be. With a prestigious full-ride scholarship in pocket, it was an offer and a destiny that I absolutely couldn't refuse.

But then I did. I've always been the good soldier and I tried semester after semester to please everyone except myself. Even with a decent GPA and a summer internship that paid well, there was something missing. From time to time I found myself drifting toward the academic buildings on campus where the zoologists were doing the things I wanted to do. On my summer internships, usually spent reading safety manuals and familiarizing myself with "standard operating procedures," I would find my way to out-of-the-way places and the Savannah River Ecology Lab, where summer students were studying birds and frogs instead of SOPs. I was growing weary of it all. And so after three and a half years of trying my best to be what others would have me be, I succumbed to the gravitational pull of my heart and changed my major to zoology. I can remember the exact spot on the sidewalk where the hard decision became an easy choice. My life changed in the moment wildlife and wild places replaced pulleys and physics. Zoology was to be my new destination.

I was suddenly happy and felt some purpose for being. The hardest courses (with the exception of biochemistry) were easy. There was stuff in the ecology and zoology texts I wanted to know. The labs weren't spent programming computers but instead dissecting things and discovering how life fit together in all of its fantastic forms. I sucked up the new knowledge like a sponge. Perhaps one of the greatest differences in the transition was my academic advisor, Dr. James Schindler. An Oxford-trained limnologist (lake specialist), Dr. Schindler saw promise in me that few others had. He insisted I call him Jim, allowed me to chart most of my own coursework, and encouraged me to pursue a nontraditional BA where arts blended with the sciences to make me a different sort of beast.

Dr. Schindler's trust and mentorship were a breath of fresh air. I wasn't another serial-numbered robo-engineering student but Drew, the bird-loving student from Edgefield who had a new lease on life. An MS (Zoology) and PhD (Forest Resources—Wildlife Ecology) followed in succession. Along with Jim Schindler, I count Dr. Sidney A. Gauthreaux, the "Godfather" of radar ornithology; Dr. Patty Gowatty, a pre-eminent ecofeminist who unraveled some of the myths of monogamy in the bird world; and Dr. David Guynn, a nationally renowned white-tailed deer ecologist, as my mentors. With each degree, I dipped deeper into the world of wild things that fed my seemingly insatiable passion for nature. Along the way, numerous friends and graduate school colleagues helped to keep me focused when the coursework got hairy or a married life with two children became a priority.

In the years since I found my true path, I've become a tenured college professor, a certified wildlife biologist, and directed hundreds of undergrads and almost fifty graduate students toward careers following their passions. I've published extensively and been rewarded with numerous awards and an endowed chair at my alma mater. It's a heady thing to be paid for your brain and being an academician means just that. It's an even headier thing if much of what you do as your job is what you'd do for free—or even pay someone else for. I've traveled to wonderful places. Along with time spent wandering across most of the United States, I've wandered around amazed in the mystery of Amazonian rainforest and pondered the seemingly endless horizons in the Kalahari. Spectacled owls, great potoos, Kori bustards, and African fish eagles are on my life list, along with painted buntings, snowy owls, Kirtland's warblers, and hundreds of other species. I've seen more birds than I would've ever imagined possible. I've even managed to expand my featherful obsession with studies of butterflies, bats, reptiles, and amphibians. Now I spend more and more of my time trying to connect the wild beings with the human ones. All of it seems to run through the idea of a Land Ethic. For that I turn to another mentor many of us in the profession call on, Aldo Leopold. I take his advice on intelligently tinkering to heart. Birds were the compass that pointed the way for me and they're still my inspiration. The investment in that Golden Field Guide, the support of a select few "believers," and all that time in the woods without a game console seems to have paid off.

If knowledge is the path we tread to get somewhere, then I think that passion is the currency that pays the toll. With my head still in the skies marveling over the ability of migrating birds to cut hemispheres in half, my heart's gamble for being something more than the expected is a wager I cash in every time I wander through spring woodland on a bird walk or sit on my deer stand in the autumn rut. I could easily call every moment in the field "work," as I piece together the interactions between wild things and wild places. For me it's easy to make the connections between white-tailed deer and warblers. It's a natural thing. I imagine sometimes what my life would've been like trying to connect mechanical things in some sort of meaningful way. Yes, it would've been the whole round-peg-square-hole deal, but much worse. I'm not so sure that had I allowed that alternative existence to parasitize my life—like some sort of soul-stealing cowbird—I would've remained sane or been much beyond someone who regretted not following the right road.

And so yes, I find myself in a special place where I'm a rare bird of sorts. In a profession that depends in large part on understanding and conserving the biodiversity of ecosystems, we suffer from a dearth of ethnic and cultural differences within our own flock. It's an odd thing and a problem we must address. I like to think about my own life history as I ponder the possibilities for conserving nature and securing our profession into the future. Like birds and other beasts, we all have dynamic range maps that flow with varying suitabilities in "habitat" or the pressures that can cause us to move or stay. Tolerance and acceptance of who we are is one such pressure, I think.

I'm a Black American doing something not so many people who look like me do. At times, others have made that more of an issue than it should be. It's been painful sometimes but mostly a joyful couple of decades deep into my career. I'm hopeful that I can serve as some sort of example for following your heart to do what it's lead to do—regardless of what the mainstream says. Look at any recent map of demographic trends and it will show a changing landscape where majority shrinks to minority and different faces will have the final say in what remains wild or perhaps what gets paved over or mined under.

Engagement and relevance have to hold hands in the effort to be inclusive. The world seems more urban, and wandering for many is a virtual thing now. And then poverty and other negative social forces all too prevalent in the lives of many people of color drive suitability to levels that challenge survival. I want that to change and to be a part of that change. Perhaps some little brown or black boy or girl is trying to find their own wings to fly. Maybe some nature-loving high school senior of whatever color is struggling with expectations that thwart dreams. I want them to see what heart means in all of it. In spite of what others told me I couldn't be, I've become just that. Sometimes you have to get lost to find your way.

ABOUT THE AUTHOR

J. DREW LANHAM *is a lifelong birder and adult onset hunter. He earned his BA and MS in Zoology and his PhD in Forest Resources (Wildlife Ecology) from Clemson University. An award-winning faculty member at his alma mater for over twenty* *years, his past research has focused on impacts of forest disturbances on songbirds and herpetofauna. Most recently, he's focused on connecting culture to conservation with a focus on understanding land ethic. A native of Edgefield and Aiken, South Carolina, Drew currently lives in Seneca, South Carolina, and lives by the mantras of "connecting the conservation dots by blending sound science, evocative writing, and a commitment to making nature matter to everyone!" Dr. Lanham is an avid poet and creative nonfiction author who communicates his love of nature with words. In addition to numerous essays and anthologies, he authored the book* The Home Place—Memoirs of a Colored Man's Love Affair with Nature *(Milkweed Editions 2016) and a chapbook of poetry* Sparrow Envy *(Holocene Press 2016).*

THE LONG DROP

Eric Lund
Aquatic Vegetation Specialist
Minnesota Department of Natural Resources

In October 2000, I descended the starboard-side rope ladder of *Rapture*, a 175-foot privately owned research vessel, and jumped into the zodiac bobbing below. Waiting for me in the zodiac was Chris, my field partner for the months to come. Chris and I had only just met a week and a half before in Honolulu, a brief period that included a week of preparations on Oahu, a flight to Midway Island, and a three-day boat voyage to our final destination by way of Pearl and Hermes Reef. Thirty minutes later, we hopped out into the turquoise shallows of Laysan Island, a 1,000-acre atoll and U.S. Fish and Wildlife refuge in the middle of the Northwest Hawaiian Island chain.

Over the next few frenetic hours, Chris and I offloaded our supplies and equipment, chatted with the outgoing Fish and Wildlife crew we were replacing, and helped load their supplies onto the *Rapture*. Shortly before sunset, Chris and I sat down on solid ground for seemingly the first time in forever (on an island that deceptively continued to sway for several days afterward) and buried our feet in the pulverized coral beach. Surrounded by the chattering of black and brown noddies and the swarms of fairy terns and Bonin petrels returning from a day foraging at sea, we watched the last zodiac navigate back out through the reef and past the breakers toward the *Rapture* now barely visible in the distance, taking with it the last people we would see for five months.

Our day-to-day duties that winter were components of a comprehensive and long-term effort to restore the island to prehuman conditions. Among our varied responsibilities were wildlife population monitoring, exotic plant removal, native plant propagation, breeding albatross surveys, and camp maintenance. To that end, our survey protocols—and our life in general on the island—went to great lengths to minimize our influence on the behavior of the native wildlife as best we could. Every article of clothing and every piece of equipment was new and unopened before it was brought ashore, or had instead spent a few days in a deep freeze in Honolulu. And fresh produce was forbidden to avoid the introduction of new pests or seeds. All of our food and drinking water for our five-month stay was contained in white five-gallon buckets and blue water jugs that numbered in the hundreds and lined the perimeter of our wall tents—these we had to patrol vigilantly to keep them well-spaced and upright in the shifting sand, lest a bird (especially one of the perpetually curious finches) wiggle its way in between the rows and become trapped.

We kept a wide berth to avoid disturbing endangered and skittish green sea turtles and Hawaiian monk seals nesting and loafing on the beach. We walked cautiously around the interior of the island throughout our tour to limit the collapse of burrows of the numerous ground-nesting bird species, and quickly worked to clear out the tunnels that inevitably caved below our feet despite our precautions.

People would ask me later if the isolation drove me crazy with boredom. But for a naturalist who embraces solitude from time to time, every minute of every day that winter was filled with wonder. Giant albatrosses returned to the island, seemingly overnight, and then performed their synchronized mating dance like an act in a well-choreographed first grade musical. Thick clouds of raucous sooty and gray-backed terns crisscrossed the sky against frigatebirds engaged in aerial robberies. In camp, mischievous little yellow Darwinian-like finches learned to open the zippers on our tents. Along the shoreline, giant monk seals lolled, grunted, and farted, or—if the time was right—gave birth. And out in the water, there were hundreds of species of showy fish I had never seen before, giant eagle rays, sharks, eels, and seemingly endless tunnels of coral reef to explore. Everything was new and spectacular. Within days of our arrival, I had taken to staying up late into the night and rising early with the sun to make the most of every day.

In the evenings, part of my ritual included a nocturnal pilgrimage along the beach to the *lua*. The lua, which we affectionately referred to as the "long drop," was a three-by-three-foot plywood box, set eighteen inches above the ground, crowned by a standard toilet seat with lid. The seat framed a hole in the box that opened into an eight-foot-deep hole in the sand. To either side of the lua were several white five-gallon buckets. Some contained rolls of unused toilet paper, but one bucket was set aside for used toilet paper, which we would periodically burn with the rest of our garbage to minimize waste and extend the life (capacity) of each pit toilet. After all, digging a new eight-foot-deep hole in the sand each year was no trivial task.

The lua we had inherited that year was surrounded on three sides by eight-foot *Naupaka* shrubs whose branches were teeming with nesting red-footed boobies, black and brown noddies, and greater frigatebirds. At the base of the shrubs, red-tailed tropicbirds, masked boobies, and other ground nesters waddled. Perched upon that plywood throne, the long drop afforded an unobstructed view over the limitless ocean that lapped the shore about one hundred feet away.

On February 21, 2001, at approximately 11:00 p.m., I made my slow, barefoot stroll up from the beach toward the long drop. A new moon meant an especially dark night, and I was mindlessly following the focused beam of my headlamp that was cast in front of my feet. When I flipped open the toilet seat, I felt a light thud against my chest. Even in that moment of surprise, I somehow knew I had collided with a bird (which, looking back, may have been attracted to, or flushed by, the beam of my headlamp). Despite all of those clumsy birds wheeling in flight around us, learning to fly and land all day and night, this was a first.

I didn't think much of the glancing blow, but when I looked down I realized that the gray-backed tern that had apparently thudded into me had crash-landed on the lua and was now tee-tering on the toilet seat, its partially outstretched wings barely spanning the opening. Caught in the glare of the stage light gaze of my headlamp, the frightened bird flopped and flailed on the otherwise empty toilet-seat stage. My heart racing, I

lunged for the bird, but not before it dropped out of sight into the abyss beneath the long drop's trapdoor.

"No way that just happened. &%@$," I said, the shock setting in.

It took a moment before I aimed my light down into the pit to get a better look at a place I had no interest in getting a better look at. Down in the darkness amid the scurry of cockroaches was the tern, flopping and rather quickly sinking into the soupy mess. Think quicksand. The more I shined my light on the bird the more it panicked, the faster it sank, and the faster my heart raced.

Feeling the need to act fast, or at least realizing my options were limited and not wanting to think too much about what I was about to do, I took a deep breath, leaned over the lua, and reached my arm straight down the hole as far down as I could, all while doing my damnedest to not touch the inside of the box.

"@#$%."

The tern was out of my reach.

Looking back into the pit, I began to panic. The tern had stopped fighting, had grown too heavy or too tired to fight, and was still slowly sinking. I began running around looking for sticks, for some reason imagining myself wielding giant chopsticks before I realized that there were no substantial woody trees or shrubs on the island. Remembering that I *had* seen a fishing net while cleaning out our storage tent just the other day, I ran toward camp, easily setting a new adrenaline-fueled world record in the one-hundred-yard dash. I found the net and sprinted back to the long drop. Back down in the hole, all I could see was little more than the bird's head.

It was only then, as I started to angle the net into the lua, that I realized *the net's metal frame was too big to fit through the toilet seat.* I would have to take the whole cover off the plywood box, which I now saw was held together by a few screws.

Back I dashed to camp to retrieve a cordless drill and Philips bit (*Please*, I pleaded, *let the battery have a charge*) and then back to the beach. A minute or two later the top was off the box. I fished around with the net and scooped up a gloppy, writhing blob that I hoped was my tern. I lifted the viscous mass out and perched it over the pit, resting the handle on either side of the box. It was dripping, oozing. I was so afraid of the mess, I wasn't sure what to do for a few long seconds. Except, there was only one thing I could do. So I turned in a half circle to face the ocean, swinging the net out in front of me, leaving behind a hyphenated arc of human crap across the sand.

And it was then that I kicked over the bucket of used toilet paper.

Naturally, the bucket lid popped off, scattering wads of soiled toilet paper fluttering across the sand in the maritime breeze. Those would have to wait.

Holding the net fully extended out in front of me, I headed for the ocean in a bowlegged waddle to avoid stepping in my own leavings. I waded knee-deep in the Pacific and lowered the net into the water, releasing a brown cloud that swirled with the outgoing current. With the next incoming wave, the brown cloud swirled around my legs. I walked side to side, rinsing my legs and the bird simultaneously until the tern began to emerge. Then, retreating back up the beach, I lowered the bird onto the sand. The tern seemed okay. Rank, but alert and breathing as normally as could be expected, given the circumstances.

I decided to leave the tern there for a minute and ran back to camp for a pair of latex gloves. But when I returned, I found the bird had disappeared. I dropped to my knees and began sniffing around under the shrubs while pawing at the sand in the darkness. By smell alone, I quickly relocated the quivering bird and scooped it up with both hands, pinning its wings up against its body. It was then that I felt the tern's tarnished feathers through a ragged rip in one glove, torn no doubt while crawling through the shrubs.

I was walking back toward camp to clean us both more thoroughly when I saw a headlight bobbing down the path toward me.

Chris looked at me and then at the bird in my hands, caught a whiff, and made sense of my situation before I said a word.

"No @#$%&@#ing way," was the first thing he said.

"Yep," was my only response.

"No way . . . Why didn't you come get me?"

"I don't know. Didn't want to wake you, maybe thought I didn't have time. Just wanted to handle my own situation or something," I reasoned. "I don't know, man."

"Well, let's clean it up."

"Okay, can you take it for a second?" I pleaded. "There's used toilet paper blowing around down by the lua like tumbleweeds."

"What were you doing with the used toilet paper?"

"I wasn't doing anything with it! I knocked the bucket over. Please just take the tern; this really involves both of us at some level. Plus you are better at handling birds anyway. I'll be right back."

At camp, we rinsed the bird off with fresh water until only a slight stench of sewage lingered. That night we stowed the tern in a plastic tote on a nest of towels heated with warm water bottles. When we checked on the tern the following morning, it seemed to have recovered.

I carried it out into the open, released my grip, and watched it fly off into the rising sun.

ABOUT THE AUTHOR

I chased, mapped, and studied the habitat relationships of rare and common plant and animal species across seven states in the Pacific Northwest and Hawaii for eighteen years after earning my BS in Environmental Science from the State University of New York at Buffalo in 1998. During that time, I worked for five different state and federal agencies and as a research assistant for several universities and was a member of both the Washington and Oregon chapters of The Wildlife Society. In June 2016, after nine years working in small, headwater streams as a biologist with the Washington Department of Fish and Wildlife, I transplanted with my family to the other side of the Continental Divide when I accepted a position as an Aquatic Vegetation Specialist on the Upper Mississippi River with the Minnesota Department of Natural Resources. I currently live in Red Wing, Minnesota, with my wife, Ashley, and our two sons, Soren and Roland.

THE $#!% I DO FOR DAVE

Katie Quint
Wildlife Biologist, Wildlife Research Institute

Hanging here at the end of a rope
on an assignment most would crave,
I cannot help but reminisce
about the $#!% I do for Dave.

"You have the coolest job in the world!"
my friends have always raved.
Rarely do they risk their lives on the job,
like the $#!% I do for Dave.

"Rappel to that nest," Dave asks of me,
while he rests, his knees to save.
I wait to cry 'til I'm over the edge,
so Dave still thinks I'm brave.

He drives us to the end of a road,
points up, and gives a wave.
Then he watches us hike through poison oak.
More $#!% I've done for Dave.

A cold front seems like the perfect time
to set up a trapping stage.
But it's hard to tie knots when your fingers are numb!
So I mutter curses at Dave.

The kick into four-wheel drive makes me cringe,
when I survey a range with Dave.
Because without fail that man always finds,
the most death-defying grade.

Hawk Watch is never the glitz and the glamour
guests see when they come Saturdays.
It's "Fix the barbwire!" or "Find us some roadkill!"
before showtime with Katie and Dave.

For that adventurous group of people who do
the same things as I, unpaid . . .
WRI volunteers, do you know why
we keep doing $#!% for Dave?

More often than not I think to myself,
"He's sending me to straight to my grave!"
But when the job's done, it's worth all the pain,
for a pat on the back from Dave.

* * *

Who is Dave? "Dave" is the quintessential wildlife biologist
who has not only committed his or her career, personal time,
life savings, heart, body, and soul to studying earth's fascinating
wild creatures, but who also inspires others to do so. If you're
lucky, you had a "Dave" as a boss. If you're good, you've *been*
that boss.

In this case, my "Dave" is cherished mentor and friend Dave Bittner, long-term director of the nonprofit Wildlife Research Institute (WRI) in Southern California. I wrote this poem after a promised "quick day of fieldwork" that involved hiking in and rappelling down a cliff face historically frequented by golden eagles to install remote cameras. We found ourselves, instead, troubleshooting the installation from sunrise to sunset on a cold-for-Southern-California fall day on the desert edge. All had gone as planned until one of the brand-new field cameras stopped working while we were testing the photo angle—the final task of the day. As I was dangling off the cliff face mid-rappel, waiting for another camera to be retrieved from our vehicles, hiked in, and lowered down to me for a do-over, inspiration found me in midair in the way of poetry.

Not coincidentally, that was also the day I stopped forgetting to pack backup equipment.

It was I dangling from that rope instead of Dave because he had long since worn his knees out, leading to total knee replacement in each leg. During his recovery, I—a young biologist—was fortunate enough to fill his shoes doing the work he loved. The only thing that pained him more than his aching knees was to sit on the sidelines while we had all the fun. Even from the sidelines, Dave's mentorship and invaluable opportunities in raptor research he gave me became the foundation of my career as a wildlife biologist. I'll always remember every one of those long field days and the countless adventures we enjoyed together doing what some call "work." I will enjoy paying it forward someday.

ABOUT THE AUTHOR

KATIE QUINT has been working in Southern California since 2011 as a wildlife biologist for Wildlife Research Institute (WRI), a nonprofit organization focused on research, education, and land-trust management. Katie has over five years of Golden Eagle research experience over which she has logged more than one hundred hours conducting eagle-occupancy aerial surveys and acted as project lead for WRI's satellite telemetry project (N=63) in California, Nevada, and Montana. She also has held an active role as a field biologist for several consulting firms, including Chambers Group, Inc.; Blackhawk Environmental; and Garcia and Associates. Katie's main focuses are ornithology and botany with a special interest in top-predator ecology, including raptors and wild felids. She shares her passion for the natural world by guiding ecotourism trips, hiking, and road-tripping. Katie also dedicates time to her yoga practice and garden.

Katie has been a member of the Western Section of The Wildlife Society since presenting on the dispersal of juvenile golden eagles hatched in Western Nevada at the Western Section Annual Conference in 2013.

SEEING SPOTS: FIELD NOTES FROM THE UNDERGROUND

Matthew P. Bettelheim, CWB
Science Writer, Wildlife Research Biologist at AECOM,
and Natural Historian

If I thought I was aimless when I applied to colleges my senior year in high school, I was certainly no better off upon graduating from UC San Diego four years later in the summer of 2000. I had aimed my sights at San Diego under the misguided idea that I could realize my dream of becoming a marine biologist because of the university's proximity to the Scripps Institute of Oceanography (the closest I came to Scripps was a seminar on mangrove swamps). Second only to my volunteer experience in the Trevor Price Lab tracking and banding dark-eyed juncos (a sparrow) on campus and in the Cleveland National Forest (that year I was detained by campus police twice—once as a reported Peeping Tom, and once as a suicidal "jumper"), my field experience was limited to an animal behavior lab in which we manipulated harvester ant-foraging strategies at Torrey Pines State Natural Reserve using different-sized food-types as bait. When it came time for me to fledge the academic nest,

I was untested and ill prepared for any semblance of a career with wildlife.

Rudderless, I followed my then-girlfriend, now-wife, Sarah, north to Red Bluff (population 13,147), the county seat of Tehama County, California, where she had landed a position as a daily reporter. At first, wildlife jobs seemed scarce. I balanced my days between shotgunning resumes to any want ad with the word "biologist" in it while hedging my bets at a local temp agency. Despite having dazzled the agency with my words-per-minute, I nevertheless failed to land a position as a receptionist. I suspect gender stereotypes may have been at work.

In my one interview at a big-name environmental consulting firm in Redding, the office manager—convinced my resume had surely been misfiled—interviewed me for an open chemist position. Not convinced that my dismal grades in basic chemistry might be in any way telltale (not to mention my outright honest assurance I didn't belong in a lab handling dangerous chemicals), I can only imagine he thought he was doing me a favor sitting me down in his office—wallpapered in equal parts religious motivational posters and game trophies—to sell the chemist position followed by a tour of the lab to set the hook. Needless to say, neither of us called the other back.

Not long afterward, I landed a position at the Turtle Bay Exploration Park in Redding. At Turtle Bay, I split my time between Paul Bunyan's Forest Camp historic re-creation exhibit and what was then their off-site natural history museum. After four years of my friends needling me about graduating into a career that entailed asking customers, "Would you like fries with that?" I was prudent enough to listen to the little voice in my head that—when asked if I would be willing to work in food concessions—told me to bite my tongue. And so, in addition to interpreting the logging exhibits and teaching visitors about the museum's resident animals—like pygmy owls and gopher snakes—some days I sold hot dogs. When times were slow, which was not infrequent, I fed pinky mice to the pair of western toads on exhibit, replayed in my head those ten seconds in which I had been fortunate enough one morning to catch a northern Pacific rattlesnake yawning (it flexed each fang, in turn, independently!), or reveled in the cunning of the museum's raven, Bosco. Feathered conjuror that he was, Bosco took unabashed glee in stealing coins from the tip jar each morning during his few minutes of free flight while his enclosure was being cleaned. From a branch atop the foam-formed faux tree house that amounted to the museum's kitschy reception desk, Bosco would practice his own David Blaine–style street magic, making a shiny nickel or dime vanish into the bottomless cavern of his beak with a flip of his head when he caught you watching him, then effortlessly make it reappear when you looked away.

In time, another opportunity arose back in Red Bluff as a seasonal scientific aide with the then-California Department of Fish and Game. For the first time, I found myself in uniform, which amounted to a patch I was instructed to sew onto a working man's desert-sand Dickies-brand work shirt. I did such a poor job with a needle, I swallowed my pride and asked my future mother-in-law to make it presentable.

It was as a scientific aide that I earned my first stripes as a field biologist. In the footprints of two proposed dams, our group was charged with conducting baseline and protocol-level surveys for California red-legged frogs, California tiger salamanders, and giant garter snakes. Night and day, on quads and on foot, we ranged into the hinterlands with flashlights and binoculars, dip-nets and seines, exploring the boonies of northern California's untrammeled lands.

The seasonal aides that came before us had left a legacy. Legend has it one crew attempted the long drive from the foothills of the Mendocino National Forest back to headquarters in the state rig during a blast-furnace summer day with the windows up and the heater cranked (a trick we dared not repeat). One day, I watched a water devil blossom and skitter across a pond we had just sampled. Another day we sampled a pond while the locals sat on a nearby fence running their mouths and polishing off cheap beer. I learned how to operate a fyke net, to back up a loaded trailer, and to execute a steering-wheel wave like a local. Walking along a dry cobble creek bed, even in the dead of night, I was as likely to encounter a wild boar as I was a pheasant or a skunk. Two of those we'd send fleeing into the night—one of those would send us fleeing for the truck. And one night I found myself walking alongside a rattlesnake who matched me slither for step down the creek, both of us looking for frogs, but for different reasons.

But during my time served, I never saw the species I set out to see. We would drive miles from the nearest town down long, aimless roads, passing gate after gate, to count invasive American bullfrogs by the thousands. I remember one beached seine haul where the belly of the net began hopping up the shore driven by a resourceful bullfrog so large, I swear he was the size of my face.

We lasted two years in Red Bluff before life demanded a change in pace. The next position I applied for—a sports fisheries port sampler with the Marine Resources Division of the Oregon Department of Fish and Wildlife—I accepted over the phone with a map of Oregon spread unfurled in front of me across the gas-range top stove. From a list of coastal cities to choose from, Sarah and I picked Brookings, based on nothing but a hunch. We gave two weeks' notice and packed up the cottage (a converted milking barn) we called home over the last two years, stowed life's nonessentials in a storage unit, and moved north with little more than what would fit in our two cars.

For the next four months, Sarah sold eyeglasses while I dragged myself up before dawn to count outgoing and incoming fishing vessels, recorded length/weight data on marine fish, and collected coded wire tags and snouts from Chinook and coho salmon and otoliths (fish ears) from rockfish. That summer we lived on the cheap, sleeping on a foam mattress, reading secondhand books gleaned for change from the thrift shop, and celebrating Thanksgiving using a moving box as a dining room table. The two pairs of pants I wore to the docks every day—blue jeans so encrusted with fish slime and blood and scales they were like plate-armor—I laundered only once, in August, all on their lonesome. Those days, quarters were prized, the laundromat was a lonely place, and I was genuinely concerned about what might happen if those biohazardous field pants came into contact with the residents of Brookings's street clothes in a soluble solution.

But the Brookings gig was seasonal, set to expire in October. When a position for an entry-level wildlife biologist opened up in the San Francisco Bay Area, I was quick to apply. At the interview, I brought extra copies of my resume, carried an extra pen, and even broke out a new pair of reading glasses acquired through Oregon's generous health care coverage to look more intellectual. The day before the interview, I read up on some restoration work the firm had undertaken in a local creek, and regurgitated it during the interview. It worked. In December 2002, I became a business card–carrying wildlife biologist. The day we moved, I threw the pants in the dumpster.

My first test as an environmental consultant came when the firm's environmental planner approached me one Friday afternoon to perform a last-minute burrowing owl habitat assessment in an open field in Brentwood. One of our clients was slated to break ground on a new medical facility there the following week. The planner had assured the client (and, in turn, me) that there were no owls on-site, and that the surveys were merely a formality.

Burrowing owls, if it isn't abundantly clear from their name, make use of ground squirrel or small mammal burrows (and, on occasion, other such opportune cavities like buckled concrete and discarded pipes) to nest in the spring and summer and overwinter in the off-season. Because they nest underground, a trait so uncharacteristic of most North American birds, there are protocols in place to make sure burrowing owls, a species of special concern in California, and their nests—both of which are protected under the federal Migratory Bird Treaty Act—can be identified and avoided in advance of any project.

Never having done a habitat assessment for burrowing owls before, I panicked. Jerry, my manager, took me aside and walked me through the assessment.

"If you can't say for certain burrowing owls aren't wintering on-site, we'll follow up with surveys," he assured me.

Standing on the project site that afternoon, I cast my binoculars across a ruderal grassland bordered to the north by a gas station and a busy thoroughfare. From my vantage spot atop a crude-cut drainage ditch riddled with equal parts mature thistles and mustards (burrowing owls steer away from tall vegetation) but also gaping ground squirrel holes, I couldn't in good conscience write it off.

Trust your gut, Jerry had told me. So I did.

The planner was incensed. "I told the client they could start work next week!" *Her problem, not mine*, I write now, although my confidence was surely wavering at the time.

But Jerry had my back. "I'll run out tonight," he offered her as a parlay, and ducked out of the office that evening to catch the sunset hours when burrowing owl activity picks up. Later that night, Jerry rang me up to say he had found an over-wintering owl holed up along the very same drainage where I had stood watching garbage tumble down from the gas station parking lot to scatter like spindrift across the nascent urgent care or surgery center.

My December start date coincided neatly with several of my new firm's ongoing projects involving protocol-level surveys for California tiger salamanders. The California tiger salamander, today a state and federally listed threatened species, is an amphibian that spends most of our Mediterranean summer underground in small mammal burrows—like those of the California ground squirrel—and emerges during winter rains to breed in vernal pools and ponds. In those days, the wildlife agencies leaned heavily on a combination of nocturnal pedestrian surveys during the winter breeding season and aquatic sampling for salamander larvae in the spring.

Much like I'd done before for the California Department of Fish and Game, I ventured outdoors in search of frogs and salamanders. In the shadow of Mount Diablo, we found California tiger salamanders during night surveys within a stone's throw of a juvenile detention facility's chain-link perimeter fence crowned in razor wire and motion-triggered floodlights. In the Dublin/Livermore hills to the south, I would fantasize how our walking transect of biologists creeping across the hummocky countryside sweeping the rain-dappled hills with our flashlight beams might look to the rare nighttime driver who glanced northward as they barreled down I-580 in the dead of night.

In Gilroy, a private developer hired us to use a fiber-optic scope to inspect every single ground squirrel and gopher burrow on a twenty-acre parcel slated for eighty-one homes to demonstrate to the wildlife agencies the absence of California tiger salamanders. In the heat of summer, we took turns putting on the Peep-a-Roo headset and draping our heads with jackets to block the sun like a parody of some nineteenth century portrait photographer. Prostrate in the parched field, with foxtails winnowing their way into the seams of our clothes, we'd thread the scope down one burrow after the next using pointed thrusts for distance and a corkscrewed wringing for lefts and rights. Exploring as much of each burrow as we could up to thirteen feet (the length of the scope), on good days we averaged 120 burrows. On bad days, we averaged thirty-six. The whole process left us disoriented and discouraged.

We had cleared 4.95 acres when, on day twelve, one of the crew—Dana, who once lived in my garage for a summer in college and would later become the best man at my wedding—gave a surprised hurrah. A mottled salamander had appeared in the viewfinder. That afternoon we got a firsthand look at the run of a ground squirrel burrow as we dug our way to that ever-retreating salamander. Forcing the shovel through the kiln-baked soil, I blew out the crotch of my tattered field pants crawling in and out of the lengthening trench, all the while juggling a mobile phone with my disgruntled client barking at me from his air-conditioned office. Much to his dismay, at the end of thirty-five zigzagging burrow feet (twenty-four straight-line feet as the crow flies), we caught up with our quarry, a juvenile California tiger salamander.

East of Mount Diablo, we canvassed one property slated for the development of a resort community and vineyards over the course of several years in search of our bread-and-butter frogs and salamanders, fairy shrimp, and western burrowing owls. At the time, the landowner was still running cattle on the property. During daylight hours, the cattle would stupidly approach our vehicles and give them tongue baths. But at night, the same herd of cud-munching cheeseburgers—unsettled perhaps by the influx of bipeds and the sweep of their flashlights—would suddenly stampede, charging at us out of the velvety curtain of darkness. In a panic, I stumbled across the bright idea of grabbing someone's flashlight and waving one in each hand like an air traffic controller to break the stampede around us, a trick that came in handy during later cow attacks.

In those same hills, I witnessed one of a pair of white-tailed kites grasp the uppermost branch of a tree limb, set its wings like a parasail, and haul back hard enough in midflight to snap the branch off as nesting material. I learned the claw-raked signs of an American badger den after one hissed at me from a shadowy hole during my amateur investigations. And I watched a property I had come to know get bulldozed, graded, and developed.

When the permitting was wrapped and construction loomed on the horizon, one of our last tasks was to exclude the resident burrowing owls. To do so, we spent weeks in a coworker's garage eating pizza and building one-way exclusion doors out of corrugated plastic drain pipe, clear plastic squares (door flaps), and zip-ties (hinges). Bundled in heavy-duty garbage bags, the finished doors were loaded into the company truck and tied to the roof rack like saddlebags until it resembled an amphibian's egg sack or a hobo with a hoarding problem or a surrealist's portrait of an overburdened donkey, then hauled them to the exclusion zones. Saddle sore from kneeling to install each door, cut by the contraption's glass-shard edges, and sodden by spring showers, there were times when—too tired to trek back to the car—we spent lunchtime napping like soldiers with our backs to the driving rain, or huddled in a badger burrow to enjoy our wet lunches out of the wind.

On one such day while hauling exclusion doors, the company truck slipped off the road precariously close to one of the salamander breeding ponds. In the weeks to come, the chain-link fencing crew would sink their truck axle-deep on a remote hillside, and then sink a second truck in an attempt to remove the first, before abandoning them both until late spring. Realizing we were in over our heads, we began calling tow-truck companies from the ridge-top (mobile phones were still in their infancy). Only one outfit in the county was equipped to take on such an off-road assignment. In return for hauling our truck back to terra firma, we mailed the operator a photograph of the stuck truck for consideration in their annual best-of dirty dozen calendar of off-road fails.

But the last task I recall from that project was the decommissioning and dewatering of the stock ponds. I had been tasked to write a salvage and relocation plan—an approach that's still considered questionable by some even today. The plan was simple: move larval, juvenile, and adult California tiger salamanders and California red-legged frogs from known breeding ponds in the project site to a neighboring pond just over the hill on newly acquired state park lands.

The plan was rejected by the permitting agencies.

To this day, I'm still in a fog about how or why the least critical parts of the plan were retained. I do recall the absurdity of standing in a stock pond as a backhoe operator breached the dam and I salvaged Sierra tree frogs and western toads from the receding waters, but then left the California tiger salamander and California red-legged frog larvae and tadpoles to bake like jerky in the empty pond bottom, legally and in accordance with the project's final state and federal permits.

That outcome never sat well with me—no matter the permits at hand. But it drove me toward clients and projects that left a lighter footprint on the land. And in those intervening years, I've matured in my career and moved on to a place in life and a place of work where I can better select clients and projects. The experience I gained in those formative years has since shaped the biologist I am today: a bit jaded, perhaps, but also wiser to the give-and-take inherent in any project that comes my way.

This year, I found myself once again on the margins of a pond, one perched like an aerie overlooking a vast, sheer watershed in every cardinal direction. This pond, however, wasn't slated for McMansions or another soulless strip mall. Instead, it had been set aside as mitigation to protect breeding habitat for special-status amphibians. We were there to monitor whether California red-legged frogs and California tiger salamanders were breeding successfully and to make management recommendations to ensure they did.

The hike down from the ridgeline where we'd left the SUV—a vehicle so lipstick-red, it drew the attention of a high-strung Anna's hummingbird the week before—was steep enough to make getting to each pond appear deceptively easy. The hike back would prove orders of magnitude worse, leaving my colleague Katie ample time to bone up on her birding (thank you, yellow-billed magpies!) while I huffed and puffed to catch my breath in increasingly shorter intervals.

After a long day of sampling ponds, we were about ready to pack it in. Each of us had caught several dozen California red-legged frog tadpoles plus an adult frog apiece. My frog had involved cat-and-mouse stalking and evasion until at last, with Katie waving her dip-net to distract one particularly slippery frog, I scooped it with a lucky swoop. Katie's frog came to her as she muttered something to the effect of, "I haven't found anything, let's call it," and made one last mechanical sweep with her net through the water, followed by a startled gasp and a bulging net. But we had yet to find California tiger salamanders, Katie's white whale since she'd started with us several months before.

After hoofing it back to the car (a trek that need not be mentioned twice), we stopped by one last pond on our way out that I knew from past years was brimming with California tiger salamander larvae—big ones. Sure enough, as we approached the pond, I spotted one through the clear water lurking in a bed of floating vegetation. I nabbed it with a flick of my net. Taking the sopping dip-net from me, Katie knelt and positioned the net in the shallows so she could examine her first California tiger salamander.

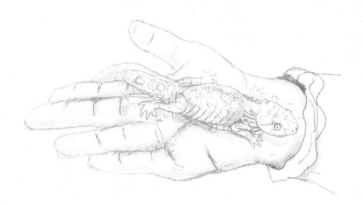

Oblivious to her excitement, I was already stewing, guilt having already set in. Katie, working under my supervision as a permitted biologist, was working toward a handling permit of her own—I should have let *her* scoop the larvae instead of cavalierly doing so myself. Give a man a fish and you feed him for a day, right?

Thinking I could channel the "teach a man to fish" motif Jerry had tried to instill in me so many years before, I told her to throw it back.

"Throw it back."

"What?"

"Throw it back."

"Oh, okay," she said, and ever so glumly but without questioning, gently released the larvae.

"Now," I said. "You catch one."

And for the next fifteen minutes, she tried to do just that. And failed. And not for lack of trying. I couldn't catch another either. For a pond that I thought was teeming with salamander larvae, these white whales had made themselves scarcer still, retreating to the pond's murky depths out of reach of our dip-nets.

As I waded deeper and deeper, grumbling and gambling my chest-high waders against the water depth and the uncertainty of each footstep in the underlying unseeable pond bottom, I was feeling like a fool. Instead of giving Katie another minute—thirty seconds, even—to familiarize herself with the larvae's markings and "jizz" (in birding, the general impression, size, and shape of an animal), I had acted rashly and told her to throw it back. The water was lapping at the top of my waders when I heard another gasp and "I caught one," at once washing away my guilt, seconds before the pond's holy water might.

Some guilt is easier washed away than others. Above my desk today hangs a facsimile of a panorama in watercolor—circa 1860— depicting the land east of Mount Diablo where I once watched that pond and its inhabitants die. I see through the overbuilt homes and manicured gardens and social-status vineyards I helped build years ago to glimpse the untrammeled grasslands and oak savannah that preceded the virulent development of California. Maybe untrammeled is too generous, given the rancheros and meandering fence and gabled stone house dotting the hills that even then had begun their creep across the landscape. Gazing into the watercolor, I imagine a time when the burrowing owls and frogs and salamanders, the badgers and the fairy shrimp—the land and its inhabitants—were still knitted together in some semblance of balance. This vista is my albatross, serving to remind me of my humble beginnings as a biologist, and my not-so-humble idea that I can put it back together again, one puzzle piece at a time.

Nature, I've found, is a humbling thing. Whether from the baptismal kiss of pond water overtopping your waders or the privilege of holding in your hand for a moment the larval materials of a California tiger salamander, its gilt-laced gills and gelatinous skin glistening as it is incrementally reassembling itself into the apex adult stage of its life, there is no shortage of awe to be found outdoors.

That is, until some fool says, "Throw it back."

ABOUT THE AUTHOR

MATTHEW P. BETTELHEIM is a wildlife biologist, science writer, and natural historian whose writing portfolio includes feature articles in outlets like Bay Nature *magazine,* Berkeley Science Review, Inkling Magazine, Earth Island Journal, *and* Outdoor California. *He also manages and writes for* (bio)accumulation, *a regional blog that focuses on the natural world as it pertains to the history and natural history of the West Coast. In 2013, Matthew authored his first children's book,* Sardis and Stamm, *a story about the Antioch Dunes National Wildlife Refuge and the endangered Lange's metalmark butterfly. Matthew is a Certified Wildlife Biologist and has been a member of the Western Section of The Wildlife Society since 2003.*

THE FIRST DAY

Joseph Drake

PhD Student and Research Assistant,
Department of Environmental Conservation
University of Massachusetts, Amherst, Massachusetts

It was ten o'clock at night. The truck was sunk to its axel. And we had an unexpected ten-mile hike out to the nearest paved road ahead of us. I could see little past the light of my miniature headlamp that was illuminating a mere few feet of the trees in the woods around me situated in the middle of a section of the largest ponderosa pine forest on the continent. And that was when we heard automatic rifle fire in the near distance. And this was my first day on the job.

Up until then, I had been working as a salesperson at a jewelry store in Indiana. Bills had to be paid. But over the last two months, I had applied for over forty wildlife jobs with little success. So when I picked up the phone one day to learn that a U.S. Forest Service position in northern Arizona had opened up—their first pick had declined and I was next in line—I had to decide whether I was ready to drop everything to report there in two weeks.

At $200 every two weeks, it was less a paid position than it was an internship. I could stay in Indiana making a decent wage, or move across the country with what would fit in my pickup truck, leaving behind family, friends, and familiarity. I had until morning to decide. I turned in my two weeks' notice that afternoon and told my folks good-bye. In four days, I was on the road.

I went west, young man that I was, rolling past mile markers on Route 66 and visiting friends from my college diaspora. By the time I reached Fort Sumner, no amount of coffee could keep my eyelids propped open. I rolled into a motel parking lot hoping to sleep in my truck but was chased off by the late-night attendant. On my way out of town, I noticed signs advertising Billy the Kid's gravesite. I followed them to a small museum building, jumped the graveyard fence to see what the fuss was about, and returned minutes later with my sleeping bag so that I could sleep next to the iron cage that guarded the old outlaw's tombstone. I awoke shivering several hours later, covered in morning dew, and was pulling away in my pickup as someone turned into the museum parking lot.

I made a point of driving in the early mornings to beat the heat because, as luck would have it, although my heater worked, my air-conditioning did not. When I crossed the

Arizona state line, the moment was ripe with clichés. The sun was rising behind me, casting long shadows across the arid landscape. The rock outcrops glowed a soft purple, erupting into a burning red. Hawks surveyed the vast range that reached to either side of the truck. Soon after, I pulled over in Winslow, Arizona, so I could stand on a corner.

It was only then that I checked my map and realized I had missed one of my must-visits: Petrified Forest National Park. I took the fifty or so miles back to the park entrance in stride and spent the entire day roaming the trails and scenic loops. Trees made of gemstones glittered in the sunlight across the Painted Desert. No, seriously. Trees made of gemstones glittered in the sunlight across the Painted Desert.

Starting to feel road and trail weary, I set out to find a camping spot. Just south of the park border was a rock shop with camping amenities where only a handful of campsites were occupied. Pulling past the giant faux-teepee that stood near the entrance (which, I later learned to my disappointment, was only for decoration and not available to guests), I chose a site and, settling in at a worn picnic table, mulled over my dinner options.

The wind had grown cold now that the sun was sinking. As I reached for my jacket in the cab of my truck, a voice snuck up behind me.

"Five dollars a night and ten more if you need electric."

I startled, and the roof of my truck and the top of head met for an instant. It was a fleeting romance that made me see stars for a moment.

"Didn't mean to scare ya' none," the voice explained as I rubbed the welt forming on my scalp. A middle-aged man wearing a bathrobe over pants and several shirts stood watching me. He had wisps of hair dancing around his head and a ten-o'clock shadow as long as the ones that had cast themselves across the highway that morning. He held a beer in one hand. Uncertainty welled up inside of me. *Who is this guy?* I thought as I nursed my smarting skull.

I asked the caretaker—as, it turned out, he was—if he could take a check. As I made out the check, he wandered off, saying he would be right back. In his absence, I started in on some gourmet (read: *last of my*) cheese and crackers and a tin of sardines. Usually, I would cook ramen noodles in a glass jar on the dash during the drive, but I had forgotten to prep that morning. So cheese and crackers it was. When the caretaker returned for the check, we got to talking about his job and I asked when the busy season was.

"Right before school starts back up." He thought carefully for a moment before adding, "Yeah. That's about right. Tonight it's just you and another kid. The other ones are just cars broke down in those spots." We chatted for a bit about the park and rocks until he ran out of beer. "I'm gonna grab another one. You want one?" He moved off to his little trailer and disappeared.

While I was waiting, I wandered over to the only other campsite showing signs of life and introduced myself to the other "kid," who was ten years my senior. I offered him one of my beers as we talked. His name was Billy, like the outlaw that had kept me company the night before. Like me, Billy was heading west for the same reason, but this wasn't his first go. He was on what he called the *tech circuit*: chasing seasonal wildlife technician positions for different parks, spending the winter in Texas and summer in California.

When the caretaker came back, his robe pockets were filled with cans of beer, and he clutched a plastic grocery bag full of beers in one hand plus an open beer in his other. I traded him my last beer—some brown bottle with a fancy name I had picked up along the way—for a Coors Light. He gladly accepted, and then gave me the grocery bag beers for good measure. "Here, kid. Have 'em, I got plenty." I tried to be polite and refuse, but he would have none of it. Instead, I split the bag with Billy.

The caretaker was a lonely guy. It became clear no one had talked to him, or had let him talk to them, for some time. The three of us drank into the night talking about everything, and little of importance. As we talked, the caretaker would amble off into the darkness now and then and return clutching another beer. Either his cans had holes in the bottom or he had, you could say, a slight drinking problem.

After one such disappearance, he returned with more than beer. "These come from my personal collection," he said, holding out his hands. "I get to help unload the big rocks from the trailers and they generally let me keep a couple small things here and there. I want you guys to have 'em." In his hands were several gemstones. Billy took a large obsidian nodule we were told was an Apache tear, while I took a palm-sized slice of agate. I think this was his way of saying thank you.

Billy was the first to bow out. I quickly followed. It was nearly three in the morning. And the three of us had finished a thirty-rack of Coors Light. Returning to my truck, I laid out my sleeping bag under the picnic table and fell asleep to the wind blowing across the range. When I woke in the early morning, I was hurting. I didn't see the caretaker again before I left, and looking back now, I can't recall whether he ever gave a name or if I simply forgot it. But I still have that rock. The kindness of strangers is a wonderful thing.

* * *

Having never been to Arizona, my preconceived notion that I would be kickin' muh spurs in the sand and stumbling between saguaros in the heat of a midday sweltering sun was dispelled by the miles of rangeland as I approached Flagstaff. Next came the climb in elevation and a drop in temperature as the snow-capped heights of the San Francisco Peaks flanked in ponderosa pines came into view.

When I arrived at the ranger station for the Kaibab National Forest, the receptionist pointed me to the second floor, where I found my boss, George, waiting for me.

"We need you to get started on some hooting," he explained, getting down to business after we had exchanged pleasantries. "Tonight we go into the field with the biologist from our neighboring forest. He leads the owl work around here, and he is going to train you on proper techniques."

Before the "hooting," George offered to get me situated in the bunkhouse. The bunkhouse was a sixty-second walk from the main office in what had once been the old ranger station. In short, it was an old cabin that had been renovated into an office and then re-renovated to house the resident technicians, firefighters, and interns. He showed me to my quarters, where I learned I would be rooming with a firefighter; handed me the keys; and left me to unpack. And fill out a pile of paperwork.

As I settled in, I felt not only nervous, but also simultaneously overwhelmed and underwhelmed. *Had I traded my comfortable life for a little shack out back on the edge of the woods?* I consoled myself that the view was quite nice from the front porch and the elevation left the air feeling crisp. It didn't seem all bad. *Did it?*

I finished the paperwork, got myself ready for the evening, and joined George at the office. We drove over to the Coconino National Forest and met up with James, where I received a crash course on the natural history of the federally threatened

Mexican spotted owl, including the owl's calls and identification. Afterward, James promised, our goal was to head into the woods to find an example of a breeding pair so I could see firsthand the difference between the males and females. We grabbed some live mice (for the owls), some water (for ourselves), and a GPS to track where we needed to go, and we piled into James's truck.

Working our way into the woods, we turned off the main road and bumped along perched across the truck's single bench seat. Along the way, James pointed out the window at the snow still clinging beneath the pines and firs. He cautioned that the snow had only recently melted off the roads, and that on the smaller roads, snowmelt and recent rains were enough to make the roads appear deceptively dry but conceal a mud puddle below that would suck a truck down.

After a dozen turns down different forest roads, James pulled off the road at an unremarkable location surrounded by a sea of trees. We spilled out of the truck, stretched our legs, and set off into the woods. The sun was low, the perfect time to mouse some owls, George had explained. James agreed and told me to try to call them in.

Mousing goes something like this: To elicit a territorial response from resident owls nesting nearby (and in turn, find nearby nests), a biologist surveying a stand of trees follows a prescribed survey protocol. Surveyors lead off with a four-note location call, a "Hoo, hoo-hoo, HOO-ah" made through cupped hands to project the call into the surrounding forest. Such calls are made in a known or suspected territory in the hopes the owl(s) will come and investigate. If no owl responds, the four-note is followed by a contact call, a long upward whistle characteristic of female owls. If and when an owl responds by swooping in and alighting on a branch, the surveyor offers it a live mouse on an outstretched branch (or hand). If the owl takes the bait, a chase ensues as both owl and biologist take flight, the biologist scrambling through the underbrush tracking the owl through the forest until it returns to its nest.

It might sound strange, but there is something beautiful about the way a silent predator like an owl takes its prey. Their wings are silent. Their accuracy is matchless. And their efficiency is uncanny as they flow from a perch to their prey and back in one effortless movement.

But that is neither here nor there. Because what came out of my cupped hands was less than noteworthy and summarily ignored by any owls nearby. "I have heard worse," offered James, "and I have heard them respond to worse too. I once got a bird to investigate a truck door banging in the right pattern." Before I could process whether or not I should be insulted that a truck door had out-hooted me, James offered up a recording of a spotted owl call.

Still nothing.

The lack of response left George and James perplexed. "They always show up," James said defensively. At James's suggestion that we try again deeper in the woods, we piled into the truck again. James launched the truck down the ever dwindling two-track. The sun was setting as we plunged deeper into the forest. Eyeing the worsening road, George said, "It's getting pretty sloppy out there."

James didn't argue. The patch of road ahead was giving him cause to reconsider his trajectory. But even as he eased on the brakes, the truck jerked to a stop and our inertia was redirected from forward motion into a sinking feeling. We abandoned the cab to assess our situation. The front tires had sunk several inches. Using a shovel from the truck bed, we braced the tires with branches and bark scavenged from the forest for traction. James was able to work the truck onto the shoulder with us pushing from behind as the mud sucked and slurped at our boots.

Having become so intimate with the road slop, we quickly realized that we had been skipping like a giant stone across the mud at high speed. It was only when we had slowed down that we lost momentum and succumbed to the mud. When James tried to gun the truck back onto the road, it simply lurched forward into the mud until the spinning wheels began digging deeper and deeper. It was a beautiful attempt but the mud won again.

What followed next was an hour of digging and bracing the tires, peppered with grunts, curses, and desperate cries of "GO!" and "STOP!" We kept at it until the mud reached the axle and the doors were scraping the mud we were traipsing through. We turned off the truck in defeat and retreated to the truck bed to catch our breath. A glance at my watch confirmed it was late. The white noise on the radio reminded us we were out of range. And cell phones couldn't pick up a signal.

It was late. We were cold. And we had a ten-mile hike to the main road in front of us. It was time to get moving.

* * *

CRACK! CRACK! RATATAT! We had hiked no more than two miles when we heard it. "Was that automatic gun fire?" George asked.

We all agreed it was.

"It wasn't that far off," said James.

We all agreed on that, too.

As we came to that consensus, the diminishing sound of gunfire was replaced by the growl of an engine approaching in the darkness. George stripped off his Forest Service jacket and stuffed it into his backpack. In spotted owl country, the local public opinion can be divided on federal employees. Especially in the Pacific Northwest, at the heart of the spotted owl controversy, it wasn't uncommon for biologists and rangers to be physically intimidated, assaulted, or issued death threats by those with a stake in the timber industry who feel put out by a bird. That mentality was not restricted to the Pacific Northwest, however. We may have been on foot and at a disadvantage, but James was no stranger to the back woods.

When at last the monster pickup with mammoth tires erupted out of the darkness, we found ourselves frozen in place like a deer in his headlights. As the truck rolled to a stop, a face poked out the driver-side window.

"Lost?" asked the face in a man's low voice.

"Naw," I shot back. "Truck got stuck in the mud."

"Gotta be more care . . ." And here the face took a drag on a cigarette and a swig of whatever was in his hand. It was a big swig. He finished off the can and a hand materialized to toss it into the bed of the truck. ". . . careful. Gotta be prepared for that. Well, anyway, I can take you as far as you like in this direction. I'm heading back to town."

Before we could thank him, the face interrupted and added, "You three gonna have to ride in the bed if you want a ride. Got the kids in the back." We looked at each other and silently agreed that it beat walking. We climbed into the bed and a sea of aluminum cans. I inspected one before the truck lurched to life. Bud Light. Every single can.

Whether he really had kids in the back seat remains a matter of debate to this day. Once our chauffeur got a head of steam, he was flying twice as fast as James had been driving before we got stuck. He was smoking and pounding beer and tossing empties out the window like it was his job. Huddled in the truck bed, I got kissed on my forehead by a lit cigarette.

Shivering with cold as we barreled along, we silently agreed we should have walked instead.

After what seemed like hours in the back of that truck, the truck slowed at the approach to the main road. We smacked at the side of the truck, hoping he might hear us over the roar of the engine and the rough road. As he slowed to turn, we took our chance and popped over the sides of the truck shouting our thanks.

"Ya sure you want out here? It's still a couple miles to town," said the face.

"Someone is meeting us here in a couple minutes," George lied.

The face shrugged beneath the dim lights of the cab before he drove off. As he swerved into the night, another beer can flew from his window and, lit by the truck's taillights, rolled across the road.

From the main road, James now had enough cell reception to reach his wife and arrange for a ride back. Ending the call, James admitted to us that he was never going to hear the end of this. He would have to call in the fire crew and a big engine to unstuck the truck. "I am never going to hear the end of this," he repeated.

Although I never saw a spotted owl that night, I would in the nights to come. Despite everything that went wrong, my experiences in the days that followed would help shape the summer that launched me into the outdoors and a career as a wildlife biologist. Resiliency and adaptation serve not only a species, but also those that study them. Sitting on the road shoulder that night, waiting for our ride and reflecting on my first evening in the field, James and George showed concern that our failure that night might scare me off until they noticed the crazy glint in my eye. Rather than despairing our failures, I was relishing the craziness of it all.

James was chuckling, and I could hear the smile on George's face as he said, "You might just make it in this field."

It has been many years since that first day, and I prove him right every day.

ABOUT THE AUTHOR

JOSEPH DRAKE is a member of the Southwest Section and the New England and Arizona chapters of The Wildlife Society. He is interested in spatial ecology, desert ecology, wildlife conservation, home brewing, backpacking, fishing, writing, photography, and science outreach. He worked for various federal agencies and universities across the Western United States (living out of the back of his beat-up Ford Ranger) and internationally in the "bio-tech circuit" for four years before returning to school to get his MS at Texas Tech University and then continuing to get his PhD at the University of Massachusetts. Keep up to date with his work or get in touch at https://secretlifeofafieldbiologist.wordpress.com/.

WINGS FOR MY FLIGHT

Marcy Cottrell Houle
Wildlife Biologist/Author

The scream came from overhead. The black dart hurtled above the ledge then disappeared in a dive to the earth. I was awake instantly. The air was cold for the third of June. I tried to dress in my sleeping bag, then gave up and jumped up half naked. The sickle-shaped flying image was gone—I couldn't find it with my binoculars because they were fogged and icy from being left out in the cold. The opportunity I had waited for all night was gone.

The falcon had left for its morning hunt. Who knew when it would be back? And I was a mile and a half from my car, camping gear, food, and water, and most of my scientific equipment. Blowing into my hands didn't help assuage the chill, so I jumped up and down, which immediately aroused the suspicions of a rock wren who apparently held title to the ledge I had usurped last night. He scolded fiercely, then paused to watch as I dressed; unlike me, the bird was oblivious of the one-thousand-foot drop-off within ten feet of us.

The panoramic view from the windy promontory was too grand to take in. It was too stark and foreign, especially when compared to the city of Colorado Springs and the life I had just left. The mountain on which I stood rose twelve hundred feet from the surrounding valley floor, and in that vertical distance the eye was taken through several vegetation zones. At the bottom were rolling foothills, pastel gray and green with sagebrush and scrub oak; then, higher, emerald forests of ponderosa pine and Douglas fir; and finally, blue side slopes of Colorado spruce and subalpine fir. I looked, as if from an airplane, at silver threads that represented rivers and at purple dots passing for lakes far below. The scene had everything—miles and miles of it—everything except people. This part of southwestern Colorado was dominated by fourteen-thousand-foot mountains. People were scarce and lived in small towns tucked away in isolated valleys.

But it wasn't people that I wanted just now, I reminded myself, with not just a hint of loneliness; it was something else, rare and unsociable—a spark of creation that preferred the highest cliffs and farthest wilderness, the fastest living creature on earth, a species that had inhabited the world for at least twenty-nine thousand years, though it was questionable if it would survive another thirty.

A startling cry, "Killy, Killy, Killy," came from below me, making me jump, and the blue, tapering wings and brilliant orange tail of a male kestrel cut through the sky almost at my feet. How peculiar, how very peculiar to see things flying below you. I must grow accustomed to viewing birds from this unusually high vantage point and to identifying them from their tops, not their undersides. Following closely behind the kestrel was a red-tailed hawk, with its russet tail fanning. Its dusty white breast and black belly band were obscured from view as it dipped down beneath the ledge and disappeared.

I threw on my down jacket and, my fingers stiff with cold, began assembling the spotting scope atop the five-foot-tall

wooden tripod. Several mule deer grazed the serviceberry
bushes on the hills below; a badger popped its head out of a
hole, sniffed the air, and disappeared again.

My empty stomach growled as I pulled on my pants. Four
months: that equated to sixteen weeks, or one hundred and
twenty days. That seemed an incredibly long time for someone
to live in the wilderness, even for one who enjoyed the adventure of far-flung places; I mustn't think about it now.

Suddenly came another sound, a whipping noise like still
air sliced by a heaving, sharpened blade. Quickly, I strained to
focus on an object moving swiftly toward Chimney Rock, the
rising sandstone pinnacle that capped the mountain and for
which it was named. I heard within seconds a cry, then a second

one in response, and through my binoculars saw two peregrine falcons racing at great speed to greet one another. Meeting it in a graceful, swirling motion that seemed but one fluid movement, one falcon flipped upside down to grasp something that the other was carrying. The bird then twisted back to Chimney Rock with its bounty while the other returned to circle above me, wailing in displeasure.

So the gamble had paid off: the peregrine had returned sooner than I expected. Once again I felt the thrill I always did for this creature, *Falco peregrinus anatum*, the American peregrine falcon. Because of its beauty, power, and courage, the peregrine has been a natural symbol of aspiration and freedom for people throughout the ages. Although I was not a falconer, I knew it was this thrill that underscored the sport of falconry, where man became as one with his bird after long weeks of training it to hunt and willingly return to him on command. The peregrine was the favorite hunting bird among falconers because of its great speed and power and the inherent docility that made it the easiest of all hunting hawks to train.

I found it difficult to fathom the antiquity of the sport. This union of man and bird had originated over four thousand years ago with the ancient Chinese; from there, it had spread throughout the world, reaching by A.D. 600, Korea, Japan, the Middle East, and Central Europe. By the year 919, falconry was already the choice sport of princes and magnates, and by the middle Ages, it became so esteemed that kings and princes kept their hunting falcons with them at all times, taking them everywhere, even to church and their own weddings. A symbiotic relationship seemed to exist between the peregrine falcon and man. Man admired the peregrine, captured it, and taught it to trust him. But at the close of the twentieth century, it was now man's responsibility to give the falcon back its freedom and its life. The alternative was extinction.

I sat down on the hard rock to lace up my boots and realized I would not have the luxury of a chair at my disposal for a long, long time. But it was worth it to me to study one of seven last pairs of wild peregrines surviving in the Rocky Mountains, by living with them during their 1975 nesting season. During this time I hoped to acquire some of the most detailed accounts to date of wild falcon behavior. I would study their life at the nesting site, or eyrie, observe their feeding patterns and hunting tactics, where they preferred to hunt and what they ate. I would record their interaction with their young and with other bird species and also their reactions to variations in weather, noise, and aircraft, and to man. From these data I hoped to document their habitat requirements and produce recommendations to aid in their management.

The fact that I was only twenty-one years old, an untested wildlife biologist straight from college, didn't seem of consequence to me, but apparently it made a difference to some people. The day before at the local Forest Service office I had expected a welcome reception when I introduced myself and asked to see Mr. Preston Fitch, an administrator involved with the project. Barry Layne, senior biologist with the Colorado Division of Wildlife and my supervisor, had explained that the peregrines were nesting on Forest Service land, and I took for granted that federal officials would be enthusiastic in cooperating with us in the study.

But upon hearing my business, the secretary's smile sunk. And, as I sat down in the lobby to wait, several heads glanced over in my direction as she passed by them, murmuring and swinging her long blond hair. After several minutes, a slight-of-build middle-aged man appeared, his chestnut eyes set in a frown. Smiling, I rose to meet him for I knew this must be Mr. Fitch.

"Barry Layne sent you?" he asked.

"Yes."

He shook his head. "Why, you can't be more than a college freshman. You're much too young for this kind of work. I will speak to Mr. Layne later today."

I had faith Barry would stand behind me, but I was still embarrassed because the secretary and several men were within earshot and grinning broadly while they sipped at coffee.

"Have you seen Chimney Rock?" Mr. Fitch continued. I answered him that I had, once, on a training trip earlier in the spring with Barry Layne and Dr. James Enderson.

"Well, in any case, I'll accompany you today. I've business to look into near there, and we can discuss what you may need in supplies—that is, if you stay."

Mr. Fitch walked briskly back to his office, leaving me standing awkwardly. His concern was understandable, but I did not appreciate the amusement of the coffee-sipping foresters. I could overhear them taking bets on how long I'd last, and when I left the office five minutes later with Mr. Fitch, their "Give 'er one week" reverberated through my ears, both as a reproach and a challenge.

Traveling with Mr. Fitch was a lesson in patience. He had insisted I go with him in the same car, which was inefficient, since it meant I had to drive back into town again, an hour away, pick up my own car, then retrace my steps. After a stop at the Job Corps Center, where he collected some camping gear, he misplaced the car keys then spent a half hour looking for them. Conversation between us was restrained; he answered my questions with monosyllables or with a grunt, as if he were crying to clear his throat. After an hour of being together, I had just about proclaimed Mr. Fitch incapable of enthusiasm about anything, but I was mistaken, for suddenly he smiled to himself as he pulled off the road to an old farmhouse.

"Why are we stopping here?"

"This will only take a minute." Without another word, he climbed out of the truck as two men approached. After a brief welcome, the three began discussing coal mining; apparently a small mining operation was located somewhere behind the house, but what it had to do with the U.S. Forest Service was mystifying. Mr. Fitch soon returned and without any explanation drove off. Curious, I asked him about the mining, and if it was on federal property. Mr. Fitch shook his head.

"Why is the government involved with it then?"

He perked up noticeably. "Because, young lady, underneath this land all around you lies something very important—coal. The entire San Juan Basin will one day be leased for coal development. Millions and millions of tons of coal are just lying underground waiting to be tapped, waiting to make this country come alive. . . . "

He paused and changed the subject. "Now before I forget, don't lose this," he remarked, reaching into his shirt pocket and producing a key. "This is for you. It's federal property, and I've recorded it in your name. It's for the gate to Chimney Rock. Only a few people have one; the road is closed to public access."

"Why would anyone try to drive up that terrible road? When I came here in the spring, we almost didn't make it to the top, it's so narrow and steep and badly rutted. No one in his right mind—"

"The Forest Service built that road," he said with pride, "and it has already cost us over a half million dollars. Unfortunately, we were forced to discontinue our efforts last year when the falcons were found on Chimney Rock."

Fitch pressed down the accelerator and, upon reaching the mountain and passing through the gate, charged up the rough road like a soldier maneuvering a tank. Mud splattered on the doors and windows, and the windshield wipers only smeared the mess. For five miles we contorted side to side, at last reaching the top, where the road leveled and dead-ended at a turnaround. Hopping out of the truck, Mr. Fitch remarked that he had no time to walk the mile to the observation overlook where I would be working. Quickly, he unloaded the water jug, portable stove, and Styrofoam cooler, which he said were on loan for my use.

"Where do you want these?" he asked.

"On the ground's fine."

"Two hundred and fifty."

"Two hundred and fifty?"

"Ruins. There are two hundred and fifty ruins here. Chimney Rock is a designated archeological district. It shelters Anasazi Indian ruins that date from the 900–1100 era."

I had been aware that Chimney Rock was one of the northernmost known residences of the ancient Anasazi Indians. They had lived in this harsh windswept land for centuries. By their ingenuity and persistence, they had achieved an astounding level of culture by A. D. 1000, surpassing all other prehistoric American Indian tribes north of Mexico. At Mesa Verde, Colorado, only a couple hours' drive from here, were hundreds of cliff dwellings that hung to cliffs like swallow nests, testifying to the Anasazi's phenomenal engineering skills. The Chimney Rock site was dated earlier, was more primitive. I was intrigued.

"Remember to stay back from the edge at the top," Mr. Fitch said as he motioned for me to get in the truck. "This creates a great deal of inconvenience. I wasn't planning on putting up safety rails until later this summer. But that was before. Before I knew about you."

* * *

By the end of that first day, I forgot all about Mr. Fitch. By the end of the second, I found I had to put aside many of the suppositions I had about life as a wildlife biologist. What you never learn in college biology class or see on television is that for every hour a wildlife scientist has actually observed his subject doing anything at all exciting, he has probably spent ten times that amount of time sitting and waiting. And waiting.

The primary qualification for a field biologist is patience. After five hours of work on my first afternoon in the field, all I had observed was

That, in my note-taking shorthand, meant:

bird left perch (⤺)
and disappeared (↖).

The art of taking field notes was something at which I would soon become extremely proficient, but at the start I had not memorized all the symbols that Dr. James Enderson and I had devised. So, at first the code did not streamline the task of recording observations, as it was meant to do. Instead, I had to write down each activity twice—once in longhand, then once again in symbols, after referring to my notes to figure out what the symbols meant.

It was a good system in theory. Instead of using the standard yellow, pocket-sized notebook carried by many biologists, I chose to fill, each day, one eight-by-eleven-inch sheet of paper, dividing this up into a grid to be covered with shorthand. On the left hand side of the paper, going down the page, were the hours of my typical observer day—0500–2100 hours. Across the page, each hour was divided up into five-minute intervals, leaving 204 little squares to be filled in with symbols. At the top of each page was a space for recording the hourly ambient temperature, wind, and, if applicable, precipitation.

HRS.	5	10	15	20	25	30	35	40	45	50	55	MIN. 60
0500												
0600												
0700												
0800												
0900												
1000												
1100												
1200												
1300												
1400												
1500												
1600												
1700												
1800												
1900												
2000												
2100												

The fourteen symbols I used denoted the major functions of a peregrine falcon's life at home:

—left perch

—flying

—circling high

—cardinal direction bird flew from cliff

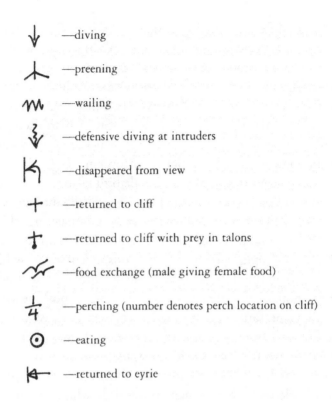

—diving

—preening

—wailing

—defensive diving at intruders

—disappeared from view

—returned to cliff

—returned to cliff with prey in talons

—food exchange (male giving female food)

—perching (number denotes perch location on cliff)

—eating

—returned to eyrie

The symbols were also color coded: blue for the male falcon, or tiercel, and red for the female, or falcon. At first I was forced to add a third color—brown—for when I couldn't tell the difference. Veteran falconers can easily differentiate between male and female birds from more than a half mile away, but I was not a veteran yet. The difference is not in coloration or general appearance. In peregrine falcons, both sexes have the same long, pointed wings, sleek and highly maneuverable; the same slate-gray-blue backs and lightly streaked white breasts; the look of pride in their sharp brown eyes; and jet-black facial markings suggesting a helmet crowning their bullet-shaped heads.

What differentiates the two is their size. Peregrines are unlike many species of mammals and birds in which the male is the larger, more visible sex. Falcons, and most birds of prey, are characterized by reversed-size dimorphism, in which the female of the species is the larger of the two. Female peregrines in fact are a full third larger and 50 percent heavier than their male counterparts and can take larger prey, which endears them to old-time falconers, who prefer them over males for hunting, and out of respect call only the female bird falcon.

The male, although an equally swift and brilliant flier, is relegated to the more unglamorous term tiercel, meaning "third."

After sitting down for most of the day, I got up to stretch and mentally made note of the first unspoken law of wildlife science: when the subject of the scientist's attention does nothing for hours, the other species of the area, those he is not recording, perform one antic after another. At least this was true from my vantage point on the exposed ledge, where more than fifty white-throated swifts were propelling themselves close by my head like miniature jet fighters in active combat. The whistle and whir of their sturdy little wings grazing past my body was more than a little unnerving, though they never actually struck me in their mad quest for insects, which also were out en masse. Hundreds of gnats and mosquitoes buzzed around my body as soon as the wind calmed and the sun began baking the cliff. And this was particularly annoying, for the one thing I had neglected to bring with me to Chimney Rock was insect repellent.

Other wildlife was quieter, but equally apparent. A yellow-bellied marmot was whistling alarm from a hole, half hidden by a blooming cliff-fendler bush; several pairs of colorful mountain bluebirds darted across the backdrop of the tall Douglas firs on the north slope; herds of elk and deer grazed in the secluded valleys hundreds of feet below.

But the peregrines were out of my sight. My pacing up and down on the ledge failed to elicit any response from the falcons, though I knew they could see me clearly. I was only a quarter mile from their eyrie on Chimney Rock, and peregrine falcon vision is superb, even legendary. With a visual acuity two to eight times that of the average man, peregrines can spot small prey from over two miles away. From their quiet I deduced two things: one, that the tiercel was probably away hunting, and two, the falcon was brooding newly hatched young and did not dare to leave them.

It was still early June, but the nesting cycle for peregrine falcons had begun weeks earlier, when the birds returned to the cliffs in late March for their yearly courtship proceedings. Usually by mid-April, egg-laying starts in earnest, extending over a period of about twenty days, when a clutch of three or four eggs is laid. Eggs hatch in thirty-three days, but in the meantime must be continually incubated. Males contribute substantially to the process. They incubate the eggs for a third of the entire time, which means that eggs are left unattended for very short periods—generally less than three minutes—while the birds change shifts. For the rest of the day, males hunt food for their hungry mates.

After the eggs hatch—the stage I suspected the birds were at now—the male spends considerably less time at the eyrie, for his attention is now directed toward searching for food for the growing brood. The female at this time is often left alone to guard the nest of helpless chicks covered with delicate white down, their half-closed eyes unseeing until they are four days old. For at least sixteen days the nestlings will mostly sleep, protected from predators, rain, and sun by the unceasing vigilance of their mother. This predictable cycle has been going on for generations of peregrines. Now it is possibly in its final stage.

Peregrines, though never prolific, were not an uncommon sight before 1940 for the keen bird-watcher scouting mountainous cliffs and river gorges. But by the mid-1970s, the American peregrine falcon, whose original range stretched from the Atlantic to the Pacific in every state of the Union, almost disappeared. Where once hundreds of wild peregrines nested east of the Mississippi River, by 1975 none remained. In the western U.S. a few residual pairs were left in Oregon, 20 or so in California, and in the Rockies, where there had been over 180 nesting pairs, only a few stragglers were left. The same tragic story was true for peregrines around the world. By 1963, their population in Western Europe and Great Britain had been cut in half; in Sweden by 1965, only 350 of the thousand pairs remained, by the mid-1970s, only four.

Yet it was not until the late 1940s that scientists around the world began suspecting things were going awry for the peregrine. By 1960, when the specter of extinction was looming over the species, biologists were racing in desperation to uncover the mysterious reason for the plunging decline in productivity, to explain why eggs were not hatching, why they were breaking, and why adult peregrines were abandoning nest sites used for generations but were not showing up anywhere else.

The breakthrough came almost simultaneously in Britain and in the United States. Derek Radcliffe, noted British researcher, after observing an ugly sight that deeply bothered him—a wild mother falcon eating her own egg—began to closely examine and compare peregrine eggshells collected in the 1960s with those preserved in collections from earlier dates. He came to the startling conclusion that peregrine eggshells after 1946 were 25 percent thinner than they normally had been.

Radcliffe relayed his discovery to Dr. Joseph Hickey of the University of Wisconsin, who in turn began analyzing thousands of peregrine eggshells in America. Hickey came to the same conclusion. Both men recognized that this single fact was highly significant in causing the peregrine's decline. Because peregrines build no nest but instead lay their eggs on rocky bare ledges, called scrapes, their eggs are under considerable stress during incubation. With significantly thinned shells the eggs are not able to sustain their parents' weight and movement, and break before they hatch.

But what was the reason for the thinning? Why was it occurring? Scientists working around the world discovered that the culprits were widely used but appalling substances, chlorinated hydrocarbons, primarily the pesticide DDT.

DDT usage became widespread after 1940. In a mere ten years' time, in a quiet but lethal fashion, the seemingly innocuous, but actually very toxic chemical worked its way up the food chain, leaving in its wake a stream of death. Small birds, ingesting insects that fed on vegetation laced with DDT poison, concentrated it in their bodies; birds at the top of the food chain, such as the peregrine, feeding on these smaller birds, inadvertently concentrated larger and larger doses of the pesticide in their systems.

At this level of toxicity, DDE, which is the first chemical produced in the breakdown of DDT, wreaked havoc on the peregrine's reproductive system. It lowered the blood level of estrogen, the female hormone, thus inhibiting the production of calcium in their bodies. When DDE reached twenty parts per million in the peregrine's blood, the falcon's eggs began decreasing in thickness by 15 to 20 percent. The eggs began to break.

Other birds, however, were less sensitive to the pesticide and masked the agent's toxicity. Ducks and gulls, for example, didn't experience reproductive failure until DDE levels were considerably higher—one hundred parts per million. But in the sensitive peregrines, when DDE levels went above twenty ppm, gruesome results occurred. The birds' nervous systems began to be destroyed. Their parental behavior went haywire. The once stable falcon began abandoning her nest full of eggs or merely refused to incubate them, so the eggs never hatched. Even worse were shocking behavioral changes such as the dedicated parent eating her own eggs.

In June 1970, the American peregrine falcon was declared an endangered species. Because of conclusive evidence that DDT was responsible for the destruction of a species, the pesticide was banned in 1972 in the United States. The interdict was hailed as a good start. But the question still lingered: Had it come too late?

Suddenly I heard the recognizable alarm call I had been waiting for, jangling me to attention. Before me a peregrine falcon emerged from the cliff with a fierce beauty; with utmost ease and perfect control, it spun in a dizzying dive to the earth. Talons outstretched, it lightly grazed the object of its attention—a trespassing prairie falcon who had slipped across the peregrine's invisible territorial line. The peregrine then bulleted to tremendous heights with an even wilder drive and, wings tightly pressed along its body, sailed again at the prairie falcon. Just before contact, however, it braked, recovering with perfect backward rolls while looping upward to the sky. Its flight was a gust of pure energy: one minute tempered, held in position, the next second a bolt of lightning striking this way and that—high, low, making mad twirls in the air—fast, slow, a crescendo of motion, and then, it was all over. The prairie falcon had retreated, and the peregrine was sitting proudly atop the cliff, surveying its world.

I slumped over the spotting scope, awestruck from the exhibition. This bird was not a ghost; it was real, and I knew that this was the place I wanted to be more than any other—living in the wilderness, surrounded by mountains, studying one of the most amazing creatures in the animal kingdom.

What I could not anticipate, however, was how severely tested that desire was to be.

I did not know, then, of the high antagonism I would be facing as a wildlife biologist, the brutal questions I would be posed, and, in the months ahead, even threats to my life. But I also could not foresee the richness of the beauty I would behold, the friendships that would enter my life, and falling in love.

Spying the proud bird again, once more I felt the truth of Dr. Enderson's words: The land and cliffs and sky can never again mean quite the same thing for one who has witnessed a peregrine in flight.

Before it was all over, it would mean something more: finding my own wings.

AUTHOR'S NOTE

This short story is excerpted from the 2014 Updated Edition of *Wings for My Flight: The Peregrine Falcons of Chimney Rock,* winner of the national Christopher Award and Oregon Book Award, by the University of New Mexico Press. It is a first-person account of those times in our nation's history when a wonderful species faced extinction. The Endangered Species Act—which two-times Pulitzer Prize–winner E. O. Wilson calls "the most important piece of conservation legislation in the nation's history"—had just been passed.

With its enactment, wildlife biologists faced dissention and animosity. Yet, as *Wings* powerfully shows, the outcome, forty years later, validates that this is a success story beyond measure.

The commitment to saving the peregrine falcon has been a joint effort involving thousands of scientists, falconers, and volunteers. Working together, their single-minded devotion has become the greatest, most cooperative, and most comprehensive undertaking to rescue an endangered species ever attempted. Today, as a result of such research and devoted recovery actions in the wake of the crisis brought on by DDT, the numbers of peregrine falcons have increased to over 3,100 pairs in North America—a number unthinkable in 1975, when fewer than twelve pairs of peregrines were known in the Rockies, and fewer than one hundred in the contiguous United States!

These stories are testaments to the indefatigable human spirit. We need to remember them, as we continue to face new challenges to our planet and its wildlife.

They show, even when things look impossible, we can—and *do*—make a difference.

ABOUT THE AUTHOR

MARCY COTTRELL HOULE is a professional wildlife biologist and an award-winning author of five books. Her articles have been published in the New York Times, LA Times, Nature Conservancy Magazine, Reader's Digest, *and* Cricket Magazine for Children. *Two of her books,* Wings for My Flight: The Peregrine Falcons of Chimney Rock, *and* The Gift of Caring: Saving Our Parents from the Perils of Modern Healthcare, *have each won the national Christopher Award.* The Prairie Keepers: Secrets of the Zumwalt *was named a* New York Times *Best Book for Earth Day. In addition, her work has been awarded the Booklist Editor's Choice, New York City Library's Best Books, and the Oregon Book Award. Marcy lives with her family on a small farm on Sauvie's Island, Oregon.*

SMARTER THAN THE AVERAGE BEAR?:
PROTECTING BEARS AND PEOPLE IN WILDERNESS PARKS

Jeff A. Keay, CWB
U.S. Geological Survey (retired)

The unsuspecting couple relaxed on a boulder, legs dangling over an eight-hundred-foot cliff. The spectacular panoramic view of cliffs and domes, coupled with the beauty of the cascading waterfall beneath them, justified the strenuous hike from which they paused to relax and eat some lunch. As I strained to shout my warning over the roar of the waterfall, they turned to look at me and then looked where I was pointing. There, inches away, a young but very bold black bear reached his salivating mouth toward the tempting sandwiches resting between them. They leaped to their feet, grabbed their belongings, and hurried off the boulder while the bear, oblivious of the blue-and-white tag in its left ear, scrambled onto the boulder and scavenged what crumbs remained.

As a former National Park Service biologist, I had devoted twelve years of my life to capturing and studying such nuisance black bears in Yosemite. A great deal of our effort during that time focused on wilderness—the part of the park that's a day's hike or more from public roads. In 1990 I left Yosemite to study grizzly bears in Denali National Park. Then, after twenty years, I returned in an unofficial capacity—as a camper (but still a biologist)—to see how things had changed for both visitors and bears. I was especially interested to learn how successful bear-proof food canisters were as the mandatory backcountry food storage device. I had watched scenes like the one above play out more times than I cared to count, and I wanted to see if times had changed.

On the first morning of my return visit in May 2009, I woke to a clear sky in Little Yosemite Valley and breathed in the light pine scent of the cool morning air. The sun still hung too low to cast its warm fingers down through the tangled branches of pine and cedar that surrounded us. Those trees had provided welcome protection the previous night when we had hurriedly pitched our tent as a loud crack of thunder and strong wind gusts heralded a brutal storm.

A hot cup of herbal tea in hand, I strolled in search of a warm patch of sun. On my way back to camp, I bumped into a National Park Service ranger. I told her about my personal connection to the park, and asked if they still had bear problems.

"Not really," she replied. "The bears I've seen over the past month haven't caused any problems or gotten into campers' food. They just seem to be passing through."

"Does the park still tag bears?"

"Only nuisance animals," she said, "and we haven't seen any of those here yet this summer."

Returning to the tent after our conversation, my mind drifted back to the morning of July 2, 1979, when—sitting behind my oak desk on the second floor of the Superintendent's

Old House in Yosemite Valley—I received a call from the park dispatcher.

"The ranger in Little Yosemite reported a small bear exhibiting very bold behavior. It's wearing a blue-and-white tag in its left ear," she'd said.

"What kind of behavior?" I'd asked. "And where is it exactly?"

"The ranger said the bear is at the top of Nevada Falls, is extremely bold, and is taking food from hikers," she'd responded. "It runs right up to people and chases them away from their lunch. He's concerned someone will get hurt."

So I'd offered to check it out.

The bear's behavior made no sense. I had captured it for the first time just four weeks earlier and placed that blue-and-white tag in his ear. At the time, the yearling—an eighty-five-pound male—had been seen searching for food in the Little Yosemite Valley camp area. But it had been very skittish and difficult to get close to.

I'd asked Brad Cella, a fellow biologist, to join me on the hike to Nevada Falls to observe the bear's behavior firsthand. There we would be joined by Richard Strong, a research assistant studying the interactions of bears and humans in Yosemite's backcountry.

The warm, sunny day had invited hikers out in great numbers. We reached the top of Nevada Falls just before noon. Small groups of hikers were perched on rocks and sprawled in the shade of tall conifers, resting after the strenuous hike and enjoying the spectacular view of the park's cliffs and canyons. The roar and drama of the Merced River charging over the brink of the falls was both deafening and mesmerizing. Many of the visitors were unpacking snacks or picnic lunches.

A little after noon, a small brown-colored bear with a blue-and-white tag—the bear we had nicknamed Yank—emerged from the forest and clambered onto the granite slab near the top of Nevada Falls alongside the visitors taking in the spectacular scenery. Quickly, and without hesitation, the young bear walked directly behind a small group of hikers sharing some trail mix. They hurriedly grabbed their food and backed away from the bear. Unfazed, Yank turned and snuck behind the next unsuspecting group. The roar of the falls drowned out the sound of Yank's approach and the outcry of raised human voices. Startled, the hikers jumped aside, leaving a sandwich on the ground. Yank snatched it up and rushed off to find another unsuspecting party. I was amazed. Yank had inexplicably lost all fear of people.

I watched Yank make his way toward the narrow bridge that crosses the Merced River just above the brink of Nevada Falls. My eyes darted ahead to survey the bridge. There sat a small boy, his legs dangling over the raging water. Too far away to do anything, I watched in stunned silence as Yank started across the bridge. The boy, his eyes widening as he realized the bear was heading for him, grabbed the bridge railing in a white-knuckled grip. Yank passed by him without paying any attention, and I let out my breath in relief. I didn't want to think about what might have happened if the boy had had a candy bar in his pocket or a sandwich in his hand.

Richard had casually approached the prowling bear to better observe its behavior, but Yank quickly turned on him. Richard backed up slowly, showing submissive behavior to assuage the bear. But Yank charged. In his hasty retreat, Richard's foot caught on a rock and down he went, flat on his back. To the surprise of both man and bear, Yank had so much momentum that he ended up standing on Richard's chest, looking him square in the eye. Richard, knowing most black bears are easily intimidated, kicked and punched and Yank bolted away.

I'd marveled at how quickly the timid bear had become bold and figured out how to obtain human food. That afternoon, back in Yosemite Valley, I'd reported the incidents to the park superintendent. Because of the high potential for Yank to hurt someone in his pursuit of food, he decided the bear needed to be destroyed. The National Park Service only killed backcountry bears when they had become a serious threat to human safety. Having become so accustomed to people at such an early age, Yank would always be a nuisance, and with the added natural hazards of cliffs and waterfalls, it was only a matter of time before someone was seriously hurt.

Little Yosemite Valley was, and still is, a popular overnight stay for backpackers. Some hike there hoping to summit the famous Half Dome the next day. Others camp there as the first stop on a several-day trek into Yosemite's spectacular wilderness. Marauding bears raided hikers' camps nightly in the 1970s and 1980s, so our team of biologists made regular trips to Little Yosemite and other one-day hike destinations. We captured nuisance bears and placed recognizable tags in their ears so that we could study the behaviors of specific bears and try to ferret out the ones that had become a threat to human safety.

Bears are incredibly curious and have phenomenal memories when it comes to food. They tear apart rotten logs and look under rocks to find food that's not readily visible; exploring for food is their way of life. When introduced to a novel object in their environment, they smell it, manipulate it with their paws, and chew it. If it turns out to be food, they remember it and where they found it. And with only half a year to secure a full year's worth of rations, they have plenty of motivation to go after any food they can find. Their digestive systems are very similar to ours, so trail food is perfect—high in calories and fats, and conveniently gathered in one place. It's little wonder they put so much effort into finding and obtaining human foods.

In those days, the National Park Service required Yosemite backpackers to stow their food in nylon stuff sacks and hang the sacks from trees using the counterbalance method. It was the only technique that seemed to work, but it had to be done just right and campers often failed. To make their task easier, we strung steel cables between trees in selected backcountry areas where good branches for counterbalancing food were scarce. Still, it was always a gamble whether a visitor could make it through the first night's camp without donating all of their food to a nuisance bear.

During those years, our team designed the first bear-proof food canisters, which were just coming on the market when

I left for Alaska. The canisters are now mandatory for back-country campers in Yosemite and many other bear parks. But the scientist in me had to ask the question: How successful are they, really? Surely there is something that fails. And, based on the amazing things I'd seen bears do to obtain food, I wondered if any would learn how to get them open.

The great success I observed in the park's efforts to keep food from bears in Little Yosemite Valley strengthened my resolve to find out how bears and humans were currently coexisting in other parts of the park; and there was no better place than the area north of Hetch Hetchy Reservoir. In this area, Beehive Meadows, Laurel Lake, Lake Vernon, and Rancheria Falls—all one-day hikes north of the reservoir—had been bear hot spots when I worked in the park years before. We had spent many nights there catching bears and cleaning up the messes they made from campers' food. What were these areas like now?

Several months after my trip to Little Yosemite Valley, I returned to the Sierras in the heat of August and was greeted by temperatures reaching ninety degrees. The bright sun ricocheted off the light-colored granite of Hetch Hetchy Valley like a reflector oven. Accompanied by family, I left the overnight parking area at midday, walked down the road, across the familiar O'Shaughnessy Dam, through the cool, dark tunnel, and up the trail toward Beehive Meadows.

I searched carefully for bear tracks as we walked down the dusty trail. Some flattened spots on top of hikers' boot tracks looked out of place, like someone walking barefoot. We slowed our pace and watched the ground intently. Suddenly, we saw a more complete track, a small pad with five tiny toe prints. These had been left by a small bear, a cub; there had to be more tracks somewhere. Farther up the trail, we saw another fresh set of bear tracks, adult size this time. Bear tracks near Beehive, just what I was hoping for.

The forest around Beehive Meadows had escaped the raging fires of the 1990s. The final approach to the meadow felt familiar, with the stringers of lush vegetation lining the intermittent creek bed amid the tall forest, and the meadows were just as I remembered them. The dense, succulent meadow vegetation stood three to four feet tall. The forest of incense cedar, white pine, subalpine and white fir, and a few scattered lodgepole pines stood tall and protective. They provided great shade from the hot summer sun and calmed raging winds during storms, creating a great camping spot. The ice-cold, crystal-clear water in the meadow spring tasted delicious and refreshed our parched lips and throats.

I searched the camp area for signs of bear activity. The steel cable from which we used to counterbalance food-sacks had been removed. No pieces of broken rope dangled from tree branches. The forest around campsites with frequent bear activity used to be littered with debris from ripped-apart stuff sacks. Bear feces in those days often contained tinfoil and plastic, telltale signs of a successful marauder. But this time I saw nothing, not a scrap of paper or even the tiniest piece of tinfoil—very encouraging.

Back in the day, Yosemite's bears were known for their persistence in devising creative ways of obtaining food. When I worked in the park, we sometimes received reports that bears strummed our steel food storage cables like guitar strings. If the paired stuff sacks weren't of equal weight, the vibrations would cause the heavier one to drop into the reach of the clever bear. Patient "beaver" bears chewed through food storage branches until they could break them. Impatient "kamikaze" bears climbed above the food in the tree and jumped, grabbing the food sacks on their way to the ground. At Laurel Lake, one of our employees watched a bear jump up into the air from the ground, attempting to reach food hung too low.

That night in Beehive Meadows, we cooked and ate a leisurely meal, spread out our sleeping bags under the fading sun, and prepared for an evening of bear adventure. We built a small campfire and told stories, staying up late to keep watch, listening for the sound of a snapped twig and keeping an eye out for any moving shadows that might indicate a bear visitor. Coyotes yipped their high-pitched yodel and several deer moved through our camp, but we saw no sign of bears. We slept under the brightest stars I had seen in a decade—so bright and numerous, I almost couldn't see dark between them. An incredible sight.

The next morning, I searched the camp carefully and saw no evidence that a bear had passed through. Our bear-proof food canisters and other gear hadn't been disturbed, there were no tracks visible, and we hadn't seen or heard anything suspicious during the night. I don't ever remember a night like that in Beehive Meadows.

With only a short hike to our next camp, we sauntered over to Laurel Lake to see if we could spot any signs of bear activity there. A man and woman reported that a single untagged bear had been near their camp for about an hour the previous evening but had not nabbed any of their food. We hiked the three-mile loop around the lake looking for bear signs and evidence that bears had obtained camp food. We found five individual piles of bear scat (feces) that contained manzanita berries and grass, and one of the piles also contained animal hair. The entire Laurel Lake area was clean—no scraps of paper and no rope stuck in trees—more pristine than I had ever seen it.

We spent a rainy night at Lake Vernon and then hiked on to Rancheria Falls. Before leaving Rancheria Falls on our final day, we checked the camps of two other groups that had spent the night there. One group had stored its food in stuff sacks suspended from a tree instead of using the required bear-proof food canisters. I walked up to the tree to examine their technique. The rope they had used to suspend the food was tied to the tree trunk. The branch was too large a diameter at the point of suspension: a small bear could easily crawl out and grab the rope and food sacks. Finally, the food hung too close to the tree trunk, easily within reach of a large bear. This was kindergarten for an experienced Yosemite bear—an easy dinner. These folks were lucky a bear hadn't come by the previous night.

All totaled, I spent four nights and six days camping and hiking in the places where we used to have some of the worst backcountry bear problems. Each of the four camp areas we examined was spotless. None of the eighteen piles of bear scat we found contained evidence of human food. Still, the abundance of bear sign was proof that bears had been keeping a close eye on popular camp areas for a free meal.

We relaxed and enjoyed this trip so much more than previous treks when we constantly feared losing our food to bears and having to abort a trip. The clean camps were also a great treat, not to mention the markedly increased safety for both bears and people. The National Park Service and responsible backpackers had successfully restored black bears to their natural role in Yosemite.

Smug in my perception of wilderness food storage perfection, I was surprised when I later placed a phone call to my friend, the late Steve Thompson, who then served as Yosemite's lead wildlife biologist. Steve informed me the park had a bear that had figured out how to open bear-proof food canisters. They had received a dozen reports of a bear near the top of Snow Creek Falls that knocked bear-proof food canisters over the four-hundred-foot cliff. The canister fragments and food trash at the bottom of the cliff were a testimony to the success of this innovative technique. One report indicated that the bear batted one canister a half-mile distance before sending it flying down the steep canyon wall. That location was subsequently closed to overnight camping when bears were active.

Caitlin Lee-Roney, who then ran Yosemite's bear management program, provided additional details. She explained that over time, the repeated use of the rental canisters loosens the metal latching mechanism, allowing the locks to slip open when bumped hard or repeatedly. The manufacturer now offers replacement parts and all rental containers in the park are regularly checked and maintained for deficiencies. Visitor diligence remains a problem too. Sometimes backpackers fail to place all their attractive items inside the canister, or fail to secure the lid tightly. These failures leave an opening for curious bears to receive a food reward, which leads to increasingly persistent efforts to explore novel ways to access the highly nutritious banquet inside the once-bear-proof, now bear-*resistant* food canisters.

We've come a long way in the last twenty years with food storage techniques in national park wilderness areas. If you overlook the rare outliers, today's bears generally behave more naturally, wilderness camp areas are cleaner and more pleasant, campers enjoy a more relaxing experience, and safety is much improved for both bears and people. Persistent vigilance is still essential, though, to protect the bears behind those ever-watchful eyes. Who knows, you might just be the camper to encounter the one who's smarter than the average bear.

ABOUT THE AUTHOR

JEFF A. KEAY *began his wildlife career working on a Master of Science degree at the University of Idaho, studying the effects of forest fires on white-tailed and mule deer. Beginning in 1978, he spent twelve years working for the U.S. National Park Service in Yosemite National Park, where he directed the black bear management program, reintroduced bighorn sheep, guided peregrine falcon recovery, and served on an interagency team to coordinate deer management. While in Yosemite, Jeff completed a PhD from the University of Idaho on black bear population dynamics. In late 1990, Jeff and his family moved to Denali National Park in Alaska, where he studied grizzly bear population ecology for the next eight years. Jeff transferred to the U.S. Geological Survey while in Alaska. He finished his career with a series of research management assignments for USGS, ending his employment as a deputy regional director for USGS in Sacramento, California. Jeff retired from the USGS in 2015 and now lives with his wife, Judy, in Idaho near Yellowstone National Park. He and Judy raised six children, none of who became biologists, much to Jeff's chagrin, but all are avid conservationists and outdoors people. Jeff continues to remain active in bear research, analyzing data and writing papers for publication. Besides his obvious passion for wildlife and the outdoors, Jeff enjoys part-time consulting and loves to guide and mentor early-career scientists. Jeff is a Certified Wildlife Biologist and has been a member of The Wildlife Society since 1974.*

BENDER SPRINGS

Joseph Drake
PhD Student/Research Assistant,
Department of Environmental Conservation
University of Massachusetts, Amherst, Massachusetts

The hike back from Bender Springs is one of the longer hikes I have in my collection. My knee and I are glad it should be the last time, too. My sore knee is a consequence of an incident involving cartwheels, something I clearly haven't mastered, and which is giving my companion something to snicker about as I graciously recount the incident to pass the time. Jordan, my plucky coworker just out of undergrad and technically my boss for this project, is keeping me company as I hobble along this blasted patch of earth. This is also one of the prettier hikes, for which I'm also thankful. It keeps the task of watching the ridges and washes for drug smugglers less tiresome. Not that we've ever seen them; only the plastic bottles and El Pato–brand tin cans hidden under the dry desert foliage left by their ghosts that haunt this section of the Sonoran Desert near Bender Springs, the only reliable water for miles.

It is late October and still the temperature reaches past the one-hundred-degree mark on my Kestrel, the handheld weather meter I carry in my pack. The sky could not hold a cloud today if a life depended on it. And it would if you were walking here without water. Thinking about the drug runners that drive stolen vehicles into this creosote and ocotillo desert until they get hung up or a blowout, and then carry on with their burlap sacks and trash bags of contraband marijuana across the desert on foot in this weather reminds me to take a drink from the bottle in the pack on my back.

Traveling on foot makes me yearn for our air-conditioned truck. It makes me uneasy when we're away from our truck as long as we've been today. Being spooked by ghosts is understandable when those ghosts are draped in camo, carry AK-47s, and pose in front of our game-camera stations cradling their guns as though they were in carnival photo booths.

As we round a corner, we catch sight of two one-ton boulders in the path—a landmark familiar to us—and around another corner, an arch on the far distant ridgeline. The valley below shimmers in the heat. I pause to rest my leg and take a photo. Ocotillos, the desert mix of a briar patch and a small tree, split the air, their spiderweb stems reaching into the sky, stretching across the desert. Thirty seconds later, we can make out the truck far below and all seems fine.

When we reach the truck, we drop our packs into the bed. Ritually, we grab a drink from the "food cooler," deposit the morning's samples in the "other cooler," and restock our supplies of vials, nets, chemicals, and bottles. Then we move on to sample the next set of water catchments, artificial watering basins placed in the desert for wildlife. To beat the heat, we always hike first, saving the drive-up jobs for later in the day.

Today has already turned out to be one of "those" days on the range. We've already replaced one of our tires, lost some critical (and expensive) equipment to the heat, and had disappointing results from the hike up top. Add to that the callous sun, a forgotten lunch, an unfortunate encounter between several spiky desert plants and bare flesh, and my already injured knee, and we are tempted to call it a day. Only good humor and a love of the work keep us in line.

We collect what data we can at the next catchment with our remaining equipment and then return to load ourselves and our gear into the pickup. The truck rumbles and the radio mumbles static. Jordan and I ready ourselves for the traverse of one of the rougher sections of the 1.7 million acres that makes up what we call the range: the United States Air Force's Barry M. Goldwater Range. After an hour of rough, slow progress, Vekol Valley Road—a high-clearance, four-wheel-drive-only road—will ease into a comparatively "easier" drive out to I-8 through the Bureau of Land Management's Sonoran Desert National Monument. Even then, it is still another thirty miles to the nearest gas station farther along the interstate.

As we approached the range earlier that morning, a new sign had been added to the accumulation of weathered signs off I-8 warning of drug smugglers and illegal immigrants. We could only assume it was important—we nearly passed it and had to put the truck in reverse to read it. Spelled out in a size-sixteen font on a sheet of plain printer paper, the sign read: "HAZARD: Road Impassable 5 Miles Ahead." The five miles came and went before we arrived at the border between the BLM land and the Range. There, a new sign had greeted us, a simple brown placard with white lettering seated atop a weather-beaten post decorated with tendrils of barbed wire that spiraled hopefully several feet before cutting short of the neighboring fence post. To those entering the range, the sign warned: "You are entering a former military bombing range. Unexploded ordnance present. Proceed at own risk of death or serious injury." And to serve as a friendly reminder of live bombs underfoot, F-16s screamed overhead. While we worked during the day, the pilots followed invisible flight corridors, releasing their payloads onto sacrificial hills just beyond the arch-topped ridge.

We begin peeling off the additional layers of clothes we're wearing as we leave Bender Springs and the range. The rocky two-track slope dictates our five-mile-an-hour retreat. Any faster and we might bottom out on the rocks already tickling our skid plates. As soon as we reach the interstate, we'll make a 75-mph beeline for a Coke and bad gas-station food.

Jordan and I have been talking about our different plans for when this field season ends. We talk until she sees me white-knuckle the wheel on a particularly worrisome section, then leaves me to concentrate on the road as she hopelessly tries to read *Jane Eyre*. The silence continues, but it is not uncomfortable. Spending four months in areas of the country where the only reception you get is Mexican "norteño" style on the AM dial has taught me to be comfortable with someone else's silence.

We reach another bad stretch of road and I try to thread the needle on a section washed out from the recent monsoons. Instead the truck slides abruptly to the right as the sand and rock collapse under the tires. Just as quickly, the truck lurches to the left as a fountain of rocks and soil erupt skyward. Time slows, but not before I hear a sharp intake of air from Jordan and I try to make sense of what—on this former bombing range littered with unexploded ordnances—could possibly have gone wrong this time.

* * *

The first time I saw Bender Springs was from the back seat of a single-engine Cessna flying over a July desert sunrise. Tim, the district's wildlife manager for the Arizona Game and Fish

Department, sat directly in front of me next to the pilot, Earl. Tim had an ex-military air about him. His athletic build was matched by his crew cut and standard-issue, day-two beard stubble. His wraparounds rested on tanned cheekbones to hide the direction of his gaze. Despite his impeccably rigid posture, behind the glasses he disarmed you with a constant smile.

Tim had been kind enough to invite me on a recon flight of the water catchments he was responsible for keeping operational. This was my second week on the range and the flight was meant to familiarize me with some of the more prominent landmarks. Halfway through our tour, Earl pointed the nose of the small prop plane toward the rising sun. We had left the airstrip before dawn to avoid the daily air traffic over the range. We had to work around the military's schedule of fighter jets, tank busters, and British royalty practicing potshots from helicopters.

After pointing out the "Dragon's Tooth," Earl corkscrewed the plane down toward the desert floor to investigate the next catchment. The plane lurched and tilted like a wooden roller coaster in the early-morning drafts, but Earl would maintain his descent until Tim called out the estimated depths of the water lines in the catchments—"Three feet!"—based on his firsthand knowledge of each one. Then Earl would pull up, straighten out, and either dodge the inevitable rock spire ahead or continue down the narrow canyon like we were bull's-eye-ing womp rats on Tatooine.

"What's that flat named?" I squeaked over the headset's com.

"That's Vekol Valley, and the silver glint along the road is the veal barn," Tim explained. "Someone figured they could raise some cattle out here at one point."

After visiting another catchment, Earl turned the plane around; we had finished our rounds and the range was waking up. It was time for us to leave the airspace before rush hour. And before the Cessna turned into a small flying oven.

Lunch, a post-flight ritual, was carried out in the truck stop town of Gila Bend at a Mexican diner named Sofia's. Tim mentioned that he was planning on visiting the area around Catchment 499 soon and would be happy to escort us out there. With the job title of wildlife manager, part of Tim's standard kit is an AR-15 assault rifle. This is because Tim is what many might call a game warden: part scientist, part manager, and part law enforcement officer. He has too many responsibilities that cover too many acres of land. Nevertheless, he reassured me he loves his job. "Where else do I get to help with helicopter surveys of antelope one day and then bust drug smugglers the next?"

* * *

When the time came to visit Catchment 499 several days later, we were joined by Steve, Tim's "super"; Daniel, one of our contacts at the Range; Jordan; and her boyfriend, Travis. Waiting for everyone to arrive, I had time to chat with Steve. Like Tim, Steve was a good-humored Arizona Game and Fish Department senior staffer who had once served as the wildlife manager in a separate district earlier in his career. His wispy, sun-bleached sandy hair danced in the equally sandy Gila Bend morning breeze.

In the gaps between the roar of passing freight cars on the tracks behind us, I explained to Steve our project—assessing the utilization and functionality of artificial water installations for game species and other wildlife. All the while, Steve attached his side arm, several spare magazines, and other tactical equipment to his bulletproof vest and waist belt with a practiced ease that I almost overlooked. Jokingly, I quipped, "Will I be needing one of those? Because I forgot to pick mine up from the dry cleaners."

Steve said, "I sure hope not then."

I squinted my face and tried hard to shrug off his answer like it hadn't been said in earnest. But before I could respond, another train roared past with four engines tugging miles of cars. By the time they had passed Gila Bend, the rest of our group had arrived, we'd split into two trucks, and we were on our way.

Tim and Steve led the group. The rest of us were piled into the second pickup with our sampling gear and supplies. The coolers squeaked against the doors. We passengers were bounced up and down as frequently as the truck lurched forward along the road.

Daniel, I learned along the way, is an RMO of the BMGR-E working for the LAFB, but often works from the

AFAF together with the AZG&F LEOs. Which is to say he is a biologist stuck in a world of military acronyms.

Despite this (but perhaps more accurately, because of this—military lands actually house some of the best and largest unbroken tracts of wildlife habitat in the United States), Daniel was almost always certain to have funding, and he was cheery every time we met. His stories that morning about volunteering with children at a summer camp and spending time with his son were typical of his good character. He is another one charged with monitoring and protecting the wildlife resources on the vast desert range. Throughout the desert, the wildlife is varied, the problems many, and the water limited. He was accompanying us that day to check on wildlife usage at these remote water sites built for large game like desert bighorn and mule deer.

We scuttled over washboard gravel until some larger dips forced us to slow and then come to a complete stop. Tim and Steve left their truck to remove a large section of brush from the wash bottom we needed to cross. The dry pebble riverbed was filled with gnarled paloverde and twisted cat-claw acacias. Long ago, the settlers of the area called this region *El Camino del Diablo*, the Devil's Road, and I began to realize why. Even in our truck, the desert felt hellish outside the window as brush squealed along the body. Our desert pinstripe—the scratches and scuffs the brush leaves behind on a vehicle (the sign of a weathered desert rat)—had already begun to appear after a week of work in the field.

Intermittently, the pickup ahead of us slowed to a stop so Tim and Steve could clear the road. But when they lurched to a halt, both officers threw open their doors with their weapons at the ready. Up ahead on the right, the grill of a broken-down maroon SUV could be seen sticking out of the brush. Tim signaled us to stop and stay low; Steve was using his door as a shield while he surveyed the area for threats I wasn't attuned to yet.

Daniel jumped out of the cab and yelled, "It's clear! That one's been cleared. Sorry, I meant to mention that earlier."

Tim and Steve eased up and climbed back into the truck.

To us, Daniel laughed and said, "Oops. Oh well, it's good practice for them!" He then explained that they'd found many abandoned cars this year. "We like to get them out of here pretty quickly so the smugglers can't use them for spare tires and other parts."

Before we could work on the Barry M. Goldwater Range, part of Jordan's and my training included learning about the dangers of the region. We learned about entry and exit procedures, venomous animals, desert plants, extreme weather, and other topics any good field biologist should know. We also learned about radio protocol, the range's unmaintained roads, its history of unexploded ordnance, its prominence as a favorite drug and human trafficking corridor, and what to do in case of UDA (undocumented alien) contact.

The seriousness of it all had not quite sunk in yet. I had grown up closer to the Canadian border than the Mexican border and the immigration issue was still abstract to me. That was quickly changing every day I drove deeper into the desert or hiked farther backcountry. I was naïve to it until Daniel began telling stories about the Vekol Valley.

A month before we had arrived, five burned bodies were found in the valley inside of a charred vehicle in what was assumed to be an act of cartel violence. There were other stories, too, plus veiled references to one instance the previous summer that Tim wouldn't elaborate on. Poking around on my own later, I learned that his casual reference concerned three separate busts by the U.S. Immigration and Customs Enforcement in 2011 that together netted seventy-six Sinaloa cartel members, 61,000 pounds of pot, 160 pounds of heroin, 210 pounds of cocaine, an estimated $760,000 in cash, and 108 weapons, among them assault rifles and shotguns.

The Arizona Game and Fish Department's unofficial policy is to never work alone in that section of the Sonoran Desert, which means working in pairs—ideally, well-trained and armed pairs. There was more to Tim's offer to escort us than to show us the lay of the land—he also wanted to make sure we survived the field season.

Organ Pipe Cactus National Monument, just south of the range and the Sonoran Desert, has become known as one of the most dangerous National Parks. It was there in 2002 that National Park Ranger Kris Eggle was killed while pursuing armed cartel members. And in the short time since Jordan and I first set foot on the range, two U.S. Border Patrol Agents had been shot, and one of them killed, along the Mexican border.

The job they do is inherently risky and I do not envy them. They are Band-Aids prescribed to cure the desert's cancer. I offer this not to belittle their service, but to illustrate the order of magnitude difference between the treatment they are able to provide versus the threats they face. The risks they take exist on an international level for biologists, rangers, wardens, and other wildlife professionals—people like Tim, Steve, Daniel, myself, and our counterparts in Mexico—whose work brings them close to the United States-Mexico border.

When we reached the trailhead to Bender Springs, we loaded our gear and set off on foot. The only sounds that broke the quiet hike were our sagging steps and labored breathing—our very own soundtrack in the still air. As we became acclimated, though, the silence gave way to relaxed talk and jokes, to reassure ourselves, perhaps, that the saguaros were not hiding drug smugglers. At one point, we followed Daniel off-trail to see a ring of old house sites. Square stone foundations and ceramic shards were all that remained of the area's original Native American inhabitants as we invited ourselves across their crumbled thresholds.

Turning off the trail, we crossed another threshold into Bender Springs. For all that the name might imply, Bender Springs is little more than a tiny little patch of mud and cattails. Immediately downstream, the spring feeds into a bedrock pool, which is known around here as a *tinaja*. The pool is hidden just out of view in a short ravine only accessible by an off-trail scramble down a waterworn granite rock face. After the hands-and-knees-descent, the tinaja comes as a shock.

The water-polished rock walls of the ravine open into a small basin that contains the tinaja. Hemmed in by rock wall, the only flat spot large enough to place yourself and a backpack was the pinch point between the two main pools. There, Jordan and I unloaded our equipment as a hot desert wind pushed past us to ripple the pools' surface. We all stood silent for a moment, letting our sweat cool our stressed bodies. In that moment, my body sighed with pleasure. I took in my surroundings until my brain had released enough steam to stop running in the red.

I started with a mental checklist of the animal life around me. I pulled out my notepad and started jotting qualitative natural history notes before we got to the quantitative analyses. The main pool was approximately eight by eight meters with three steep, smooth sides. The fourth downstream side, low and built up by the game wardens to help hold more water in periods of drought, opened to the drainage below. At the pinch point between the pools, we watched a trickle flow between the two pools; the spring was just barely keeping up with the rapid evaporation. Farther downstream, where the ravine was filled with paloverde, cholla cactus, mesquite, and other prickly brush, we would not have made a single mile an hour in that direction.

We pulled out our scientific doodads and gizmos to record various environmental parameters, including water quality. Our audio-recording device, a vital survey tool known as an audio-logger, was broken on the hike in. Travis took off in the heat to return to the truck, where our spare waited. While he braved the midday sun, I used a densitometer, a small wooden box with a concave mirror inside, to check the amount of shade and canopy cover. We would use this information and much of the other data gathered for evaporation modeling used in an ecological study of the waters. I inched along the edges of the pools using only handholds until I found a good spot for my feet. I had to hold on with one hand at all times or risk tumbling into that muddy tub. I wrenched the densitometer out of my back pocket, flipped it open like a sixties sci-fi communicator prop, and took readings at each cardinal direction around the pool.

After recording wind speed, temperature, vegetation data, and basic chemical analyses, we stopped for a drink before moving on to observe and record any wildlife in the area.

Why put so much effort into sampling a water hole? All this work might seem like a fool's errand, but there is a practical reason for this application of taxpayer funds.

Ignoring for a moment the philosophical and sometimes controversial explanations based on wildlife's inherent rights to exist and our society's moral responsibility to help offset our impacts on their existence, big game animals bring in a large amount of money to state governments. Water in desert areas can be scarce, and natural pools like Bender Springs even more so. The Arizona Game and Fish Department and various federal agencies have worked together to place more artificial catchments in dry, desert areas to help big game and other wildlife species not just persist, but thrive. During many hunting seasons, these catchments help create a slightly artificially heightened population that then can be culled by the American sportsman.

In addition to the taxes sportsmen pay when they purchase guns and ammo, there are other profits realized by guides and outfitters, room and board, and outdoor gear sales. But one litmus test that clearly demonstrates sportsmen's willingness to invest serious cash is the sales price of game tags sold at auction. In 2008, one sportsman paid $67,500 for the chance to shoot a single pronghorn antelope (another western desert denizen). But the record for this type of game tag auction is held in Montana, where a bighorn sheep tag sold for $310,000. In Arizona alone, the total revenue from these special tags was $19.5 million dollars between 1984 and 2011, amounting to an average $720,000 annually. This money is usually used to fund more conservation projects, like the water catchments. Which explains why every catchment we visited had a faded, bullet-riddled sign that read, "SPORTSMEN this development was constructed for your game with your money. Help protect your investment."

As we worked, we checked the ridges overlooking Bender Springs in hopes of seeing some of the big game that might visit the catchment, but saw none. Meanwhile, Jordan sampled both pools with a dip-net for aquatic invertebrates. Later, we spent hours peering through a dissecting microscope looking at the differences between minute body features to identify the specimens we'd pickled in a sterile alcohol-filled vial. The make-up of invertebrates inhabiting a water body is a good indicator of environmental health on a local scale. Generally speaking, because different species are able to tolerate different environmental conditions, the presence and absence of certain animals can be used to evaluate environmental health. However, in a remote and isolated desert spring, it becomes much less clear-cut; a species' absence could instead be attributed to the site being too far-removed to have been colonized in the first place. But then again, nothing is clear-cut in this desert landscape.

After Travis returned with a working audio-logger, we ran around after dragonflies like mad men, attempting to capture and count the multiple species that frequent these waters. Travis had devised a clever slingshot method, while I jumped back and forth armed with a butterfly net. I felt like a frustrated six-year-old chasing these annoyingly perceptive organic orni-thopters. Blue-green darners, flame skimmers, and spot-winged gliders hovered just out of reach in a jeering taunt of, "Oh, whatcha doin' down there, hun? Looks interesting for sure, but I gotta go. Bye!" and then they tore away to hover over the cen-ter of the pools and scoop up insects like little hawks.

As we packed the survey gear and stowed the samples, I looked again at the trickle flowing between the pools. Little black bodies—*Stratiomyidae* fly larvae—had worked their way against the current in an attempt to reach the upper pool. The hundreds of tiny dancers flailed back and forth, writhing and flexing tissues to meet the demands of a behavior instilled in them from millennia upon millennia of sunrises and sunsets across the desert horizons. A flow of water two inches wide kept them protected from the dry desert as they wriggled. These lar-vae would grow to be the soldier flies that buzzed around our head and bit our necks, endearing themselves to no one but the predators that feast upon them.

The *Stratiomyidae* are an integral part of the ecosystem here. Strangely enough, I later realized, they also mirror my own desert experience: moving between pools in spastic pulses, only working on a different scale. A different scale, perhaps, but the result is the same. As desert dwellers, we share the common problems of water and predator. When the spring stopped flowing enough to keep that trickle alive, the whole place would change until the next rains.

Either you make it or you don't.

* * *

Rock grates on metal. Acting on instinct, I realize my boot is trying to push the brake through the floor ineffectively. The truck reels and then settles. Instead of the screech of hot metal tearing away our truck and the silence of post-apocalyptia that should follow, there is neither. The truck, Jordan, and I come to rest at an awkward tilt and relief replaces my momentary pang of fear before it is quickly edged out by a feeling best described as pissed-off.

In what was the most dramatic five-mile-per-hour blowout I have ever seen, the desert has just chewed through another tire. Thankfully we had been warned and were carrying an extra spare for just an occasion. This wasn't the first time we had to use both spares in one day during our field season, either; this epic blowout marked the eighth tire we had sacrificed to desert rock and air force shrapnel during our short four-month stay.

Halfway through switching the tire in the least precarious spot we could hobble our truck to, I realized that the last three miles of road had eaten two of our heavy-duty tires and we still had at least twenty miles to go. If we got stuck again, we would have to decide whether to sit and wait with the truck or hike out to either the interstate or a spot of cell phone or radio coverage (both highly unlikely until we neared the interstate). If we waited, we had extra water for at least a day without being uncomfortably dehydrated. But waiting assumed someone would come looking for us, which also assumed someone had registered our entry to the range and that a second someone would notice when we didn't sign out at the end of the day. And if we choose to walk, we had that same amount of water for the hike out through Vekol Valley. Under either scenario, we'd spend a lot of time in Vekol Valley by ourselves. Not the most desired outcome.

Since our initial visit to Bender Springs, we'd gotten too comfortable and our respect for the desert had begun to drift with the sand over time and through repetition. Now, the boogeyman of Vekol Valley was reasserting itself. Every rock in the road became a possible traitor and every bump a new nemesis. It was slow going. Driving at half the normal speed only increased our anxiousness to drive faster and leave the desert behind us. five mph . . . ten mph . . . five mph again . . . an exultant fifteen mph . . . . STOP!

Every time we hit a good stretch of road the speedometer would race wildly back and forth and our progress would stall to a crawl by washes that appeared from nowhere. After many miles of yo-yoing progress, the silver glint of the abandoned veal barn, whose welcome rafters stuck into the air like cattle bones around a water hole, rose like a mirage on the horizon. From here the road improved and we were close to the interstate.

When we finally hit the blacktop, it was without further incident. That is how it goes out here in the field. Mostly dull with a 10 percent chance of terrifying. The desert is entirely and utterly unpredictable, and will rip out your throat just as soon as you turn your back. Respect it and it may let you leave. Don't, and you're unlikely to get a second chance.

* * *

When the field season was over, I made my way eastward in search of my next position. But I still miss the magic of the desert. When the sun sets, the desert pauses for a moment as the inhabitants transition from a mode of raw survival to a reprieve of simply being. Humans and wildlife emerge from their dens to mingle under a sky whose softening fabric, worn well enough to let the stars shine through, drapes over the landscape. The heat can be forgotten for a moment as a light breeze slips through from some far distant corner like a sigh. The wind carries itself beyond your own oasis and moves on to comfort the others sharing the same forgiving night.

The desert cares little for national boundaries or skin color or job titles or other human constructs. All it asks is for your respect, and even that carries little weight beneath the blazing sun. But this is the price we must pay if we wish to return to the desert to unlock its secrets and experience its magic. Only then can the desert cast its spell under which some of us fall in love. I fell in love with my little patch of sun, sand, saguaro, and stones at Bender Springs. Even that, though, was not enough, for either of us.

ABOUT THE AUTHOR

JOSEPH DRAKE *is a member of the Southwest Section and the New England and Arizona chapters of The Wildlife Society. He is interested in spatial ecology, desert ecology, wildlife conservation, home brewing, backpacking, fishing, writing, photography, and science outreach. He worked for various federal agencies and universities across the Western United States (living out of the back* *of his beat-up Ford Ranger) and internationally in the "bio-tech circuit" for four years before returning to school to get his MS at Texas Tech University and then continuing to get his PhD at the University of Massachusetts. Keep up to date with his work or get in touch at https://secretlifeofafieldbiologist.wordpress.com.*

THE BIGHORN SHEEP DE-WATERING DEVICE—
SPECIES RESTORATION
IN DESERT HABITAT

Thomas A. Roberts, CWB
(June 6, 1947–November 24, 2017)

On the San Bernardino National Forest (SBNF), we had a population of desert bighorn sheep, maybe two hundred or so, that drifted here and there through the varnished rocks of the mountains south of Palm Springs, occasionally showing up on some movie star or ex-president's lawn to drink from the swimming pool and eat up expensive ornamental plants. Ignoring this propensity to associate with the rich and powerful, the bighorns are astonishingly resilient and resourceful animals, willing to make a living in terrain that would kill a mule deer or a crow. There aren't even many coyotes out there, and coyotes can survive on shirt buttons and morning dew.

A week without water in midsummer is no big deal for the bighorn. They can eat thorns you could hammer through a two-by-four and run up cliffs with ledges invisible to the naked eye. And the males, of course, settle their rivalries by throwing themselves at each other like smallish, supercharged locomotives going in opposite directions on the same track. Tough.

But in the 1970s their ranks began to thin. The reason, like so much in this business, was a mystery worthy of Sherlock Holmes. We knew from carcasses and from watching them hawk and spit that lungworm was rampant, as well as a particularly nasty disease called bluetongue, one of those world-class viruses that have slashed and mauled their way out of southern Africa. But we didn't know whether these bugs were the cause or just weapons wielded by something else—after all, both bugs had been around for a century.

We did have some clear evidence that the habitat had changed, not so much in the mountains as down in the Coachella Valley. The fields of perennial bunchgrass and the stable waterholes that had carpeted the valley floor were now golf courses of franticly irrigated coastal Bermuda grass (cut shorter than a sheep could chew) and a few stylish ponds of Colorado River water made noxious by fertilizer runoff. The cutback on food and water, and the exiling of the sheep to the hillsides made their mountain oasis particularly important. So the Forest Service and the Bureau of Land Management (BLM is the government agency that gets the public land nobody else wants) had constructed a series of rainwater catchment devices—"guzzlers" in trade talk—to make up some of the loss. Now the SBNF is widely regarded in the Forest Service as an urbanized forest, an island surrounded by the ever-rising tide of Southern California humanity. These drinkers, however, were in isolated spots by anybody's standards, ten or fifteen nukes from any road or trail, over surrealistic black-and-blue escarpments dotted with cholla and catclaw. The washes between the escarpments had steep and crumbly sides and bottoms, a bouillabaisse of brambles and boulders. No one ventured there except the sheep and the odd desperate character such as dope growers and real estate speculators, and we did our work by helicopter.

In 1982, we inventoried the guzzlers and found all of them messed up in one way or another. The aprons that collected the meager rain were often torn up by the sheep's hooves, and the pipes, which ran from the storage tanks to the actual drinking troughs, were cracked by the intense sun or the periodic hard freezes of winter nights. I therefore planned an extensive and enjoyable project for the fall of the year (the start of federal fiscal year 1983) to go out and fix them.

Fiscal year '83 was when the ax fell on my program. We had been waiting for Reaganomics with a universal expectation of doom and we were not disappointed. There was no budget. I mean no budget at all, for wildlife work. I accepted this stoically, although I stopped calling myself, and registering to vote as, a "Teddy Roosevelt Republican," and began to look around for other ways of doing business. One source was the Youth Conservation Corps, a federal job program that met the administration's desire to put lazy slum dwellers to work. That took care of labor, but aircraft costs and supplies were another matter. I ruminated over this for a time, then remembered that at least one of our guzzlers, called Guadelupe after its neighboring canyon, had actually been constructed on BLM land by mistake. I called Terry Russi, a tall-drink-of-water wildlifer for that agency, and asked what he had in the bank. One of the few advantages in working for BLM is that they were so poorly known that the Budget Office hadn't been able to find them yet. So the next week, we flew out on one of BLM's ships and talked about how we could conspire to fix Guadelupe before the fall rains or BLM's turn at the fiscal bloodmobile, whichever came first.

Guadelupe Guzzler was on a ridgetop above the canyon, with a vertiginous view all the way to the Salton Sea. Terry was a desert-loving biologist and an expert on sheep. He argued that, BLM land or not, the structure was in the wrong place. He pointed out sensibly that sheep do not look for water on ridgetops, where there never is any, but in the canyon bottoms. He said he would pay all costs excluding labor and paperwork if we moved the installation downhill. "You're absolutely right, Terry," I replied, with the unctuous readiness of a poor relative. "But what about the apron and the storage tank?"

"No problem," he said, waving his hand out over the five-hundred-foot drop to the canyon bottom. "Just run the pipe on down, and keep the rainwater collector up here." I agreed, because it was August and the day was starting to get too hot for me to think clearly.

This was my first mistake.

I'd taken a course, as all Forest Service people do, called Basic Wildland Firefighting, and I knew that the water pressure increase down such a fall of slope would blow out the float valve at the trough, if not the pipe itself. But I also knew of a wonderful invention called a pressure reducer designed for such a situation. We struck our bargain and the week after our reconnaissance, armed with a secret BLM charge account number, I drove into LA and bought five hundred feet of super heavy-duty plastic pipe and two of the largest reducers made, massive bronze fittings the size of lunch boxes.

Thus equipped, I made my plans. We would shuttle in a full crew of YCC, sling-load the gear, and be out again the same day. The operation would be complex and demanding and require precise timing: Terry was getting rumblings from the BLM office in Indio that he was to be transferred to Bishop and his Southern California desert program would be "consolidated" (abolished). We were close enough to the line that an extra day or two, or camping the crew out, would result in BLM's pulling the plug on the project.

We met—BLM, FS, YCC, and my adoring blond-haired assistant, Connie—on a flat spot outside of La Quinta where desert motorcyclists changed oil and dust problems were consequently minimal. Despite a somewhat grungy heliport, littered with blown tires and Pennzoil cans, it was a splendid morning. The YCC crew had been doing scut work all summer. The hardcore streetfighters had been weeded out, and when their van arrived, they were pink and scrubbed and eager. This would be their first copter ride, first backcountry project, and their first time out with the legendary T.A. Roberts.

The sun was just slicing over the canyon rim, with the surgical precision of desert mornings, when the BLM contract chopper swooped down with Dan Tyrell at the controls. Dan was widely regarded as The Greatest Helicopter Pilot in California, and he looked the part. He routinely flew for wildlife studies and rescues, perching on one skid over impossible cliffs to drop off capture crews, chopping off rotor tips in heavy logging slash to rescue hypothermic hikers, and appearing regularly in *LA Times* feature articles. He was not only a phenomenal pilot but a fully certified mechanic who did all his own work, the owner of his own company (hence able to indulge a taste in Chivas Regal), and blessed with the ability to remember the names of everybody he ever met. He had hair the color of stainless steel, cleanly etched features, and a perpetual tan. His manner was always calm and amiable and everybody loved him, myself included.

I was a little uneasy around Dan. The last time we'd flown together, I had forgotten something critical (I forget what) and had to go back for it. Then I'd forgotten my lunch and had to eat his. It's just aggravating as hell to look stupid in front of helicopter pilots, especially when they are endlessly affable. Especially when this one was The Greatest Helicopter Pilot in California.

But all went well, at first. We zipped out in four loads, alternating between people and material, according to a schedule I'd worked on for several nights, so that arriving personnel would have exactly what they needed to get started without waiting for the next trip. Everybody went to their assigned chores with a sense of competency, purpose, and the worthiness of our enterprise. We had the collecting apron replaced by coffee break (I'd brought coffee for everybody in large thermoses marked *coffee*) and the new line laid from the apron to the storage tank by lunch.

Hooking into the storage tank, I had my first reversal of the day. The outlet was an old iron gate valve that was cracked and leaking badly. I'd planned for this, of course, but as I checked each of my carefully labeled boxes, I fought a panic that rose like bread dough in my stomach. Although I had bushings and nipples of all sizes and shapes, adapters and bell reducers and clamps, washers and hacksaws and PVC dope and a bottle of champagne to christen our work, *I had forgotten the gate valve.* I now could see it quite clearly in my mind's eye, snug in a little box (carefully labeled) on the front seat of my pickup truck in La Quinta.

There was nothing to do but swallow my pride. At $300-an-hour flight rate, and an hour-and -a-half round trip, I'd have to find $450 somewhere to pay for my mistake. It was doable, just barely. I walked over to where Dan was talking to Connie and made my confession. Dan was affable as usual, but Connie's reaction bothered me, laughing in a sisterly fashion and tossing her hair to catch the sun. Did I detect a slight diminution in her adoration? Or worse, a slight shift in allegiance to Dan Tyrell? What was she doing talking to him, anyway? Although I had no romantic interest in Connie whatever (except a teensy bit), she was the last person on the District who knew me and still believed I could do anything and knew everything. This blind, unreasoning faith got me up in the morning sometimes, and kept me limping through District meetings tedious enough to kill.

When Connie asked to go along with Dan, I knew the jig was up.

"Tom, I know just where the whatchamacallit is, and I can save Dan time when we get there."

Oh, right, I thought. *I'll bet.* But I said "okay" and smiled self-deprecatingly. Now that I thought about it, she'd been stealing glances at him all morning. Dan roared the ship off the ground like a kid pealing out of a parking lot, and I could practically hear him say affably: "Wildlife biologists are great guys, but real space cases, don't you know," as they zoomed down the canyon.

I kept everybody busy enough to barely notice when they got back, 92.5 minutes later.

We were now into the major effort of the day, the five-hundred-foot line down to the new trough. Every inch had to be covered by slabs of rock to protect it from the sun (you can't bury pipe when there's no dirt), and for three hours we labored like Chinese on the railroad—scurrying up and down slope, breaking and hauling rock, holding each other on the steep scree by belts and shirttails, fighting pipe that writhed like a python and burned like pot handles on a hot stove. The YCCs loved it, God bless them, and kept saying things like, "Bitchin' project!" and "This is the kind of thing I signed on for!" which restored my self-esteem a little. I could live without Connie, I decided, if six streetwise Angelinos found in me something to admire and respect.

But we'd fallen behind schedule and it was getting dusky in patches when we had the system ready to test. Dan's helicopter, which had been off on another mission of daring or mercy, had returned for the first load out, so I sent everybody back to the ridgetop to begin ferrying out. They lined up along the ridge, seven figures backlit by sunset, dirty and tired and proud of what they'd done, waiting for me to perform the final adjustment so Connie could break the champagne bottle over the holding tank. From my vantage, about halfway down, I could see both of them and the trough at the canyon bottom, but they could only see me.

The final adjustment was to install the pressure reducers. These had huge hexagonal collars on the intake side to hold the pipe against the force of the water. I had the biggest pipe wrench I could find for the job, and I approached the first reducer with it slung over my shoulder like Paul Bunyan with his ax. They were all watching me; I was onstage. I lit a cigarette and called to Connie: "Get ready to test!" She walked over to the new gate valve.

The pipe wrench was not big enough to tighten the collars.

I mean it was a big wrench all right, but the collars were humongous, the size of my spread hand, and there was no way I could move them. Struck dumb, I stood and stared at the locking collars, gleaming malignantly in the desert sunset. No torque, no grab; no grab, no pressure reducing; no pressure reduction.

I would have the equivalent of a water cannon, the kind they'd used to blast away half of the Sierra Nevada Mountains during the unforgettable era of hydraulic mining. "Say when!" Connie called brightly. Behind her appeared Dan Tyrell, looking outstanding in his leather flying jacket. Beside her were the YCC youngsters, standing proud.

What would you have done? I could lie, of course, and no one would ever know except me. But the sheep, unless they came by for a quick shower in the ten minutes or so it would take to empty the tank, would get no more use from this than they would from a wrecked airplane. I could tell the truth, and have everybody think I was a total geek. It was too late to go back, and there was no money for another round trip anyway. I toyed with some wilder options, like trying to start a forest fire and calling in Air Attack, banging on the collar with rocks, opening the valve at the top just a crack instead of all the way, honorable suicide. Then the sly demons of Rationalization dropped by. "Well," they said, "in the first place, the pipe is super heavy-duty and the reducers aren't really necessary. In the second place, these kids, these ghetto youngsters, look to you for leadership, a role model. They need to know that some-where in the world people don't take drugs and hang out all day, and that what they do makes sense. In the third place . . ."

"Say when!" Connie trilled again. Now Dan had picked up the bottle of champagne and stood ready to break it on the good ship Water Tank.

Miserable, I waved my hat. "Let her rip!" I shouted, and rip she did. At the first collar (where I stood) there was just a serious hissing scream of a leak. At the lower reducer, two hun-dred feet farther down, there was a lovely, lacy halo around the inlet pipe, and a rainbow ten feet across. And at the drinking trough itself the float valve, unprotected by the reducers, blew out with a report like a rifle shot. It's a good thing no animal had put its head in there—it would have been decapitated.

"How's she look?" the YCC Crew Boss called.

"Great," I replied, filling with self-loathing. The crew all cheered and danced up and down.

I'm not really that weak and miserable a human being. What I had decided, in the second before waving my hat and shouting, was that I would return on foot to this spot within the next month, hike in from Indio with the biggest pipe wrench in Riverside County. I would do this on my own time, some weekend, and only me and the sheep would know. How hard could it be to find this place from the ground? I stayed down below the ridgetop until the last load lifted out. I had Dan do a 360° around the spot, and thought, *No sweat.* Just down the canyon from the trough there was a spectacular three-hundred-foot cliff that would make an unmistakable waterfall when the rains began, and at its lip was a rare cottonwood tree. No way I could miss that.

This was my second Big Mistake.

* * *

It's amazing how large pipe wrenches can get. Before I acquired an interest in the subject, I had a rudimentary notion of their structure and function, but only few are privy to the majesty of the pipe wrench in its full glory. The one I found, after ransacking the District's tool sheds for a week, reached slightly higher than my belly button. On my bathroom scales (my son asked, "Why are you weighing a pipe wrench?"), it checked in at eighteen and a half pounds. The jaws were as large as the head of a banjo.

Two weeks after the unhappy adventure at the guzzler, I headed back in, past President Ford's house and Bob Hope's house and even the last Homely House of Frank Sinatra, through the date groves south of Indio, where the illegal immigrants ran and hid like flushed quail, thinking my whip antenna and door emblem belonged to *inmigración*, past the end of the tracks where the dune buggies turned around. I went on till I mired axle deep in sand. I locked the truck and left a note on the windshield, not so much because I had any concerns about wilderness travel alone as to eliminate confusion if anybody came by. I'd been in on enough pointless rescue efforts—"I wasn't lost, Ranger; I just met this great chick"—to make sure no one got prematurely worried. Of course, no one was likely to be looking in the right place anyway. I'd told my wife I was going fishing in Baja and the dispatcher that I was counting deer pellets at the other end of the District.

I checked my gear. I had a gallon canteen, which weighed an arresting nine pounds but was enough water only if I could get more. We'd had a rain shower and I was pretty sure of finding some along the canyon route I had charted. Sleeping bag, flashlight, matches, tarp, and the newest Travis McGee novel. I had two full days' worth of food, and enough for a third night in a pinch. The staples included the Kraft Deluxe macaroni and cheese, which I liked all right and which was cheap and filling and needed no milk or butter to make; granola and dried milk for breakfast, which went back to the days when I was a Colin Fletcher disciple; lunches of crackers and peanut butter removed from Forest Service fire rations; and a fifth of Cuervo Gold tequila decanted into a quart plastic bottle. It's a matter of great pride among us professional outdoorsmen never to touch the tasty and convenient freeze-dried foods now universally available. It's also a matter of pride to be able to make oneself comfortable no matter how hostile the surroundings. My fire building, shelter construction, and culinary skills were all rudimentary, but I had discovered—courtesy of my boss, Jerry, who also introduced me to smoked rattlesnake—that if you camp with Jose Cuervo, you don't really need any of those skills . . . although it's wise to bring along more aspirin than you might otherwise.

Then, of course, I had a three-foot-long pipe wrench weighing eighteen and a half pounds.

This made a considerable load to be carting through the desert heat. I would gain almost two thousand feet before the Guzzler, to an elevation where autumn had established itself; but in the broad, trackless mouth of the wash I cut a strange figure, if not for the mountainous pack then for the wrench strapped across the top and making it impossible to walk through the scattered tamarisk groves. It was one of the small miracles of this story, that, after staggering through the sand for a very long hour, I was overtaken by a beautiful young woman wearing a black bathing suit and riding an enormous Percheron horse. I recognized her instantly as the moll of one of the District's most notorious marijuana growers.

Although the San Jacinto soils are not especially conducive to pot growing, Timothy Leary had spent some time wandering these wastes, and our resident cultivators remained out of loyalty. Forest Rangerhood in the eighties acquired a certain paramilitary flavor as we tried to root these people out. In fact, the first briefing I had as a new hire was in the identification of antipersonnel devices. Dope growers can be dangerous brigands, no doubt about it, but they have a high tolerance for eccentricity when their gardens are not nearby. The woman seemed to recognize me in a faint but friendly way (I was not in uniform, of course) and said simply: "Hop up and I'll take you in a couple of miles." The hopping up part was hard but the horse carried us easily until the terrain got rocky and started to rumble up toward the Santa Rosa Crest. She smelled of perfume and sweet lady-sweat and she never asked why I was hiking in the desert equipped for industrial plumbing work. Good omen, I thought.

The rest of the day was lovely, windless but cool. The cliffs of the mountains rose above me on both sides, burned black and smoothed by the sun. I was walking in deep shadow by 3:00 p.m., except where a lateral canyon carved a notch and the light slammed through. When the sun set, these bright diagonals had a russet hue, like they were coming through stained glass. I reached the base of my cliff as the show ended. I looked up and located my reference point, the cottonwood tree at the top. The headwall was an impressive sight from below: it was too early in the season for a waterfall, but there was just enough trickle over the edge to spread out and moisten the whole climbing surface with blotches of algae. It looked like a wall plastered with lime Jell-O. It gave me a moment's queasiness to contemplate the ascent, but I was a man with a purpose and I made my camp, preparing for a final assault the next morning.

There was a dead ironweed tree at the base of the fall. Ironwood is the best firewood imaginable and provides the rare luxury of a completely smokeless fire. I ate macaroni and cheese and drank coffee and tequila and stretched luxuriously

out on the sand. I pulled my boots off and dried my sweaty socks by the fire and filled and lit my pipe. As if that weren't contentment enough, at last light I saw a sheep, a young bighorn ram fifty feet above me on the canyon wall. Sheep are not afraid of people if they are above them, since no predator can match them in vertical escaping skill. He was there until it got too dark to see.

The sheep was gone when the light came back. I tidied the camp, buried the fire, and strapped the wrench across my back. I settled my cap squarely on my head and strode to the cliff face. Nothing that rope and pitons and a crew of experienced climbers couldn't handle, I thought, and started up.

It was a grueling and terrifying climb made ten times worse by the weight of the wrench. It kept working its way loose no matter how I strapped it; then it would hang down by the line from the hole in one end, so that if I leaned to the side for a handhold it would pendulum out in a fearsome, remorseless arc. It was too low to smash my fingers, but the line usually grazed my knuckles and tried to pry my fingers loose. It would then swing back with equal malice and crack my shin. If it worked loose when I was going straight up, it would lockjaw into some small crevice or around the stump of a bush.

When the sun had been on my back for an hour, the metal heated up and it was hard to hold for more than a few seconds. The twenty-third time this happened I whipped out my knife and prepared to cut the monster loose. Through sweat-stung eyes, I saw the blade descend and paused. "Why am I doing this?" I asked myself. There were all kinds of cosmic answers but the one that arrived came wrapped in Connie's complete faith in me and in the glowing faces of the YCC crew, and in the vision of the thirsty sheep. I was doing it to fix the lousy pressure reducer, which I had screwed up. I put the knife away and got a grip on myself, if not on my eighteen-and-a-half pound iron counterweight.

Who wants to live forever, anyway?

Around one in the afternoon, I reached the base of the cottonwood tree and scrambled over the edge, triumphant. The watering trough wasn't there.

Not only that, but farther up the canyon I could see another cliff over two hundred feet high, with another cottonwood tree at the top. It looked so much like the first one that for a wild moment the past hours seemed to have been a dream, and that I was just waking up in camp after too much tequila. But no, there they were, one cliff below me and one above me.

I was not as anguished as I might have been, having just stared Death in the face and so on. At least now I could be assured of where I was, because there was *absolutely no doubt* this had to be the right cliff. It was thus in a positive frame of mind that I ate my lunch and drank the last of my water, only faintly troubled by the thought that waterfalls and cottonwood trees were more common in the desert than I'd expected.

I took a brief nap, then approached Cliff No. 2, a prelude made more interesting by the stand of catclaw acacia barring the base of the rock. This plant has billions of perfectly hooked thorns on every branch (its African cousin is appropriately called the wait-a-bit bush), and seems to have been designed by nature to tear clothing and skin into slivers small enough to fertilize the soil. Mother Nature, however, had not reckoned on a determined man with a three-foot pipe wrench, and after yowling and swearing my way into its clutches, I showed it who was boss. When I started to climb, I was pleased to find I'd learned much from Cliff No. 1. I rigged a better harness for the wrench and stripped to my skivvies for greater flexibility. I left my canteen behind to save weight. I climbed the wall with the proper courtesies to the Basalt Gods, and with much the same attitude as a house painter climbing a ladder, and my feeling of conquest was only slightly dampened by the fact that the trough was not at the top of this one, either.

Calm down! Don't get upset. If the cliff with the guzzler is higher in the canyon, you would have had to climb these two anyway. No time lost, really. I trotted ahead to where the canyon turned and there was the familiar sight of a cliff-and-cottonwood. Now, however, it was getting late. If I climbed this third cliff and fixed the guzzler, I would have to either climb down in the dark or bivouac in my skivvies. If, on the other hand, I went back now, I'd have to climb and descend Cliffs No. 1 and 2 all over again.

And what if, *what if,* I had taken the wrong branch of the canyon before I camped the night before? What if one of those lovely side canyons was actually the right one? This last possibility was so revolting that I knew instantly it had to be correct. I was in the wrong canyon.

I remedied this by climbing out of the canyon entirely, and trying to get a better look around from the adjacent ridge. The climb up was almost as bad but without the lime Jell-O, and the view was marvelous: canyons of every description stretching off in every possible direction, with a delightful smattering of cottonwood trees. We got canyons enough for everybody, I started to cackle—big ones small ones fat ones tall ones. Canyon, canyon, who's got the canyon. *Pull yourself together, boy!*

My situation was growing more fascinating by the minute. Now I didn't have clothing or water, hadn't fixed the drinker, *and* I was still a long pull from camp. My best course, I decided, was to leave my clothes and canteen in the acacia patch and try to work my way around the cliffs by staying on the ridgetops. An excellent plan and I started covering ground in a hurry. I was tired, but a sunburned man in his underwear can't easily sit down anywhere in the Sonoran desert, so I kept moving. I had some trouble getting back to my camp canyon directly, so I chose to zip down into a side canyon that accessed it before it got too dark to see, and I spent a whimsical hour or two going the wrong way in the right canyon. I regained camp—food, tequila, Travis McGee novel, caffeine, nicotine, and sleeping bag—shortly after moonrise, and it was ten minutes before I realized I was still wearing my pipe wrench.

I will spare the reader the details of the next two days, except to say that I got more confused and disoriented. I never got back my clothes and although there was enough water at camp to drink, I neither washed nor shaved. I went rapidly from frustration to despair to a sort of crazy fervor. For three days, I wandered through the desert like some kind of demented, messianic plumber, wielding my pipe wrench like Moses did his staff. On the morning of the third day, climbing my seventh cliff in my third canyon, I came across the skull of a bighorn on a little ledge at eye level. It brought me to my senses. I was beaten.

* * *

It was so good to get back to civilization that I didn't start feeling miserable for a couple of days. "God, you look great," everybody said. "You've got the best tan I've ever seen, and you've lost weight. Where on earth did you go, a health spa?" But the horrible truth of my failure waited patiently for the hoopla to die down, then informed me in a soft, serious voice that I was an extraordinary idiot, that I was pathetic, and that the animals of the forest deserved better than me.

It was the time of year when Civil Service requires all employees to be rated on performance, and when my turn came, I refused to accept anything better than a mediocre.

This greatly confused Jerry, my boss, who in twenty years in the Forest Service had never had anyone request a lower rating than was offered.

I wouldn't tell him why. I didn't tell anybody anything. In fact, I largely stopped speaking, period. I grew a beard and sat morosely in my office all day. Connie quit the Forest Service about two weeks after I got back and got a better paying job selling secondhand clothes in Desert Hot Springs.

There is no reason why I should have been rescued from this situation. There was nothing I had done to deserve it and I was simply lucky, maybe a more important trait than most people realize. But about ten days after Connie left, the front desk called down to say there was a woman from the Bureau of Mines to see me. "She needs to talk to Jerry; I don't do mines," I said.

"I think you should talk to her, Tom," the receptionist said with the slow, deliberate, tactful efficiency that holds the U.S. Government together (where do we get these excellent people, anyway?). "She wants to fly into Guadelupe Canyon, and didn't you have a sheep project out there this fall?"

I knew the tide had turned when Angela walked into my trash-cluttered, smoke-filled office (the one with the giant pipe wrench hanging from a twenty-penny nail) and wrinkled her nose in involuntary disgust. She looked something like Connie and something like the girl in the bathing suit with the Percheron horse. She was a geologist surveying for tungsten, out on the desert end of the District. She wanted to overfly some canyons, among them Guadelupe, and wondered if I could help, maybe even fly out with them? She had a helicopter. "Where?" I asked.

"Why, outside," she said. I looked out my window. By God, there was a Hughes 500 (not Dan's ship)—a fast, quiet, perky little chopper, parked over by the fire station. I turned back to her and stared, hesitating the way a drowning man might hesitate to grab a rope, for fear it'll be an illusion.

"Can I bring my pipe wrench?" I asked.

She looked at it appraisingly. "What's it weigh?"

"Eighteen pounds, seven ounces."

"Sure."

I had her drop me at the guzzler while they refueled in Palm Springs. It took me all of five minutes to scramble downslope and tighten the collars, open the valves, and watch the trough fill with cool, sweet water. When I got back to the station that afternoon, I confessed everything to Jerry.

"I can't remember," I said. "I positively cannot remember ever having done anything as stupid as this."

Old Jerry leaned back and pushed a plate of smoked rattlesnake toward me. He raised the coffee cup that was permanently welded to his wrist and took a sip. "Don't worry, Tom," he said. "You'll probably forget this one, too."

ABOUT THE AUTHOR

THOMAS A. ROBERTS *authored two Edgar Award–nominated mysteries:* The Heart of the Dog *and* Beyond Saru. *His life as a wildlife biologist became the source for two collections of natural history essays:* Adventures in Conservation *and* Painting the Cows. *Tom was a Certified Wildlife Biologist and longtime member of the Western Section of The Wildlife Society since 1974.* Tom Roberts passed away on November 24, 2017, at the age of seventy.

THE TOWER COLONY

Brianna Williams

Graduate Research Assistant, Southeastern Cooperative Wildlife Disease
Study and the Warnell School of Forestry and Natural Resources,
University of Georgia

Between the summer of 2013 and spring of 2014, the tower
colony on Middletown Island had been something of an obsession. As a graduate student at the University of Georgia in the
summer of 2014, I had just begun the journey of studying the
effects of disease on shorebirds. Specifically, with my involvement in the Warnell School of Forestry and Natural Resources'
parasitology lab, I had become interested in the effects of ectoparasitism on the fledging success and health parameters of
nesting black-legged kittiwake chicks. The seabird colony on
Middleton—a remote island in the Gulf of Alaska—was where
I had been assigned to look for answers.

That first year in graduate school leading up to my field
stint I spent researching Middleton Island. In the 1950s, the
United States Air Force constructed the air force station there
to conduct surveillance on potential Soviet Union attacks on
United States soil during the Cold War. It was decommissioned
a decade later due to budgetary restraints, leaving behind the
defense station's structures to slowly rust away from exposure

to the damp, salty sea air. But even before the island was proposed for a military base, scientists had recognized Middleton's importance to breeding seabird colonies. As many as ten different species of pelagic (open-ocean) birds (seven of which I planned to study) flocked to the island's high cliffs and sand flats during the summer months to mate and nest each year, making it an ideal breeding bird stomping ground.

Before I left Georgia, I could locate the skeleton of every broken building on the map hanging on my cubical wall. I traced photograph after photograph with my eyes until I was convinced I had walked among the rubble and over the marshy fields myself. However, little of my preparation and sterile research could begin to prepare me for the experience of living and working in the middle of a seabird colony on a remote Alaskan island.

The day I departed Anchorage for Middleton Island was one of those clear, sunny days that happens approximately once a year in Alaska. I was still recovering from the harrowing twelve-hour trip from Atlanta a few days earlier. Nearly my entire trip, including the hours I was accustomed to it being dark, the sun had shown its face, highlighting a beauty I never expected to find in Anchorage, the largest city in the state. As I jumped on a small Piper PA-31 Navajo hopper plane with my mentor and my volunteer technician to begin two months of fieldwork on the remote island, the weather had reached a peak of perfection, with temperatures in the mid-sixties and only a few wisps of clouds overhead. The unfettered views from the window brought to mind the opening credits of an imaginary arctic remake of *Jurassic Park*. We flew over mountains frosted with snow and dotted with glaciers out to the expansive beautiful blue-gray ocean where, as if we were part of some storybook, whales peeked out of the waves to welcome us to the island. It was only after an hour of travel over the open water that the tops of the Middleton cliffs became visible. The excitement in the cockpit was nearly audible. Our arrival marked the return of the buzz of human life to the island, where we would be spending the next two months.

Imagine an odor between that of an industrial poultry operation reeking of feathered bodies crowded into a small space mixed with a winter beach, ripe with old seaweed and stale seawater. That is what assaulted our nostrils as we exited the plane, the pungent perfume of thousands of seabird nests. The island itself was a barren marshland, nearly devoid of trees, except a few lonely remnants standing vigil on the south end of the island. The main means of transportation, as we soon learned, was a fifteen-year-old all-terrain vehicle, which was started with a rusty pin and a silent prayer. Alternatively, we could traverse the five-mile-long stretch of road encircling the island on bicycles with more rust than brakes.

We got to work the moment our feet touched the gravel runway. After off-loading our equipment onto a rusted trailer attached precariously to the aforementioned ATV, we began running trips to one of the air base radar transmission buildings to which we would become quickly acquainted. This building was the common area for field crews that normally inhabited the island from April to October. This year, my miniscule crew of two and the biologist who had been working on the island since the early seventies would be its sole occupants. The chateau, as it was lovingly named tongue in cheek by famed French ornithologist Etienne Danchin, was a damp one-thousand-square-foot structure that housed supplies; a basic kitchen; pantry leftovers, such as decades old condensed milk, seemingly endless amounts of granola bars, and industrial vats of beans, all of which had been stored in a closet for years; and a hodgepodge of discarded furniture to be enjoyed during what little downtime could be found. For years, it had been haphazardly decorated with the remnants of the small things picked up by past field crews: a colorful rock here or a tiny bird skull there. Each item a ghost of the former individuals that walked, studied, and lived amid the peeling walls of the quaint building. At one point, the chateau had stood as the main telecommunications headquarters for the Middleton Island Air Force runway, but its role had been repurposed after it was reclaimed by field crews over the years.

After a quick lunch seated around the chateau's massive kitchen table, at last we climbed the steps of what had become my obsession over the last year: the tower colony. The tower was, in the Air Force station's heyday, the main radar tower used for incoming flights. After the base was decommissioned in 1963, as the abandoned tower succumbed to the elements, it began attracting unsuspecting kittiwakes and cormorants to its cliff-like cement skeleton. Soon, the tower had become a highly sought-after nesting site. Biologists, recognizing the unique opportunity the tower presented, capitalized on the tower structure by building nest boxes to further attract birds to this prime real estate. In doing so, they created an unparalleled environment for seabird research. And so, from within the tower, we could cross that thin line between man and nature to study the hundreds of birds that were otherwise so far removed from human contact. Because these birds return to the same nest year after year, a behavior known as nest fidelity, researchers like us were allowed an extended and intimate glimpse into the lives of this colony, a connection most bird researchers are unable to enjoy.

To reach the nest boxes, we had to brave a distressing climb up three flights of sea-rusted steel stairs whose landings had long since dissolved and had been replaced by ancient two-by-four boards scavenged from the carcasses of neighboring buildings. Despite my fear of heights—the thought of falling to the unforgiving concrete foundation below terrified me at first—I grew accustomed to the one-hundred-foot climb up those rusty stairs four to five times a day. At the top of the stairs, it narrowed into a short passage of enclosed concrete before opening into what would be my joy and despair for the foreseeable future.

The experience of coexisting in the middle of a living seabird colony is indescribable to those who haven't lived it. Having become Middleton's centerpiece over the years, the radar tower was anything but unremarkable. The tower was a predictably rounded structure that had been carefully partitioned into two floors—really, wooden landings—in the tower's upper levels. Each landing was surrounded by nest boxes stacked three tall and nine across, arranged like outward-facing shelving exposed to the elements. Each nest box could be accessed from the tower's interior through an internal one-way sliding glass door. Strangely, the birds of the Middleton Island tower colony were aware but mostly indifferent to our presence.

Despite our daily intrusions, they continued their routine of incubating, feeding, grooming, and defending their summer homes in the time-honored tradition of raising the next generation. The colony was thus a flurry of parents coming and going to retrieve food for themselves and their offspring, chicks pushing their damp heads through their eggshells into the world for the first time, and birds without nests or young vying earnestly for future nesting locations. A seabird colony pulsates with activity, giving you the feeling each individual is a miniscule component of an immense, complex, and singular life-form. It was into this colony life that I became quickly absorbed, becoming a modest cog in the machine.

Every day, several times per day, after the first (or often third) cup of coffee beginning early in the damp morning, I climbed the tower colony, my tired technician trudging behind me. Our attire consisted of heavy, awkward yellow rain gear, suspiciously reminiscent of a certain frozen fish salesmen. These slickers were meant to protect us not only from the onslaught of the nearly ever-present rain, but also from the nonverbal protests of birds that disliked being handled, and from bird-fleas unwittingly seeking a meal from the wrong taxonomic order of hosts.

Once in the tower, we fell into our routine of counting the survivors from the previous night and welcoming the new hatches into the world, methodically working our way around each landing until our sample collections were completed. Our sampling included a cloacal swab, several basic morphometric measurements (e.g., wing length, tail length, weight, tarsus measurement, and head-bill size), and a quick blood draw as the prize golden ticket critical for molecular sampling, which was to be conducted back in the home laboratory in Georgia. Each data point was carefully recorded on data sheets: a hieroglyph untranslatable to the outsider and yet sacred among field biologists. We broke for lunch every day around noon and then returned to the tower to fish for parents with the highly scientific protocol of a curved coat hanger hopefully hooked around a leg before they could disappear from the nest with a flash of the wing. We repeated the same measurements for parents with the questions of age differences and infection status weighing on my mind.

In the evening, when the sampling was done, we would trudge down those now mundane stairs away from the constant squawking of fighting parents and the mewling of hungry chicks and relish the silence. There, for a moment, we could regain perspective of our own humanity separate from that of the tower colony that had taken us in.

The days ran into each other, marked only by the changing weather. And change it did. Often. In the span of a week, I spent one day on the beach bathed in sunshine and light beads of sweat on my forehead, while on another I laid awake for fear my poorly staked tent would be carried off by gale winds as a storm cast down upon the island a frigid torrential rain. The next morning, as that terrifying storm broke into a soft drizzle, I made my way to the tower to investigate. Many of the young chicks, too small to cling to the nests, had been swept away by heavy winds in the night. That day, feeling so much a part of the colony, we mourned alongside the parents who brought back the morning's catch to a now empty nest.

I would often return to the tower alone right before bed, a last vigil to revisit those chicks that had lived to see the end of another day, and to straighten the mess that comes with a busy day of work. It was in these moments when the sunlight filtered through the hundreds of tiny nest windows, splashing intricate patterns of dying light across the floor reminiscent of some ancient cathedral, that the colony would become quiet in its own way. Much like the beating heart right before bed, it still pulsated, but in a calm, almost to the point of mute, stillness. The parents, done with the constant trawling of the day, and the chicks, bellies full from their parents' labors, settled for long naps. Each bird in their own way was battening down the hatches to survive until the next morning. It was in those moments of quiet reflection that I felt closest to the tower and the colony living within it and to my own research. Breathing in the unique colony air, I would leisurely muse over my drive to understand this colony and to figure out the smallest intricacies of the birds' existence and my own role in that continuation.

As it came to a close, I found the last two months—from the first chick I handled to the close of the nesting season—a dizzying whirlwind. Exactly fifty-two days after our arrival, we boarded an emergency flight and departed Middleton Island on a squally day so unlike our incoming journey. It wasn't until I was back in that cramped cubicle in Georgia that I had time to reflect on my first field season. Now, far removed from the colony, I sit for hours instead at a lab bench, poring over the samples we worked so hard to collect day after day. But it is those quiet moments alone with the birds that I relive in my daydreams. As I remember the equal parts isolation and inclusion I felt in their world, it reaffirms the purpose in my research as I strive to bring myself a little bit closer again to my tower colony.

ABOUT THE AUTHOR

BRIANNA WILLIAMS received her bachelor's degree in Forest Resources with a Wildlife Biology and Management emphasis from the University of Georgia. While completing her undergraduate degree, she began conducting wildlife disease research at the Southeastern Cooperative Wildlife Disease Study (SCWDS) on three blood-borne parasites in African carnivores. She came back for round two as a double dawg and is currently pursuing a PhD from the Warnell School of Forestry and Natural Resources in Wildlife Biology and Management. Brianna's doctoral research focuses on the health of a breeding population of six species of seabirds located on Middleton Island, Alaska. Specifically, she is conducting a survey of a variety of blood-borne pathogens, the role of avian influenza maintenance in seabird breeding grounds associated with convergent waterfowl flyways, and experimental effects of ectoparasitism on nesting black-legged kittiwake chicks. While the health of seabirds is Brianna's current research focus, she is passionate about the research and management implications of all diseases affecting wildlife and domestic populations. Outside of research, Brianna enjoys sharing a life with her husband, Philip; their two dogs, Molly and Bella; and their orange cat, Eliot. Brianna is affiliated with the University of Georgia Student and the Southeastern Chapters of The Wildlife Society and is a member and Student Representative of the Wildlife Disease Working Group at the national level.

GRAND PATRONS

INKSHARES

CPSIA information can be obtained
at www.ICGtesting.com
Printed in the USA
BVHW031101111219
566316BV00001B/112/P